Perpetual Wealth
First Edition

First published August, 2019

Copyright © 2019 Ethan Galstad
All rights reserved.

Permission is hereby granted to freely share and distribute this book (in whole or in part) by educational institutions for the use of educating their students. All trademarks, servicemarks, and company names are the property of their respective owners.

Author's Notes:

This book consists of my opinions. I am not a financial advisor and do not recommend any specific course of action with regards to your finances or investments. As in all things in life, make your own decisions and choose carefully. Unless specifically stated otherwise, names, characters, places, ideas, and events are solely the creation of my creative imagination. Individuals and companies mentioned in this book did not endorse the content or concepts of this book.

Perpetual Wealth

Other Books In The "Zero To Hero" Series

Other books in the "Zero To Hero" series are listed below. Be sure to visit https://zerotoher.co for updates on new publications.

The Book Of Us:
How What We Seek, See and Perceive Defines Us and Our World

This book offers new perspectives on society, belief systems, and relationships.

Profiting From Fear:
How To Leverage Emotions, Exploit Weaknesses And Make A Killing

This book offers unconventional wisdom that turns the table on the old rules of marketing, sales, and making enormous profits.

Perpetual Wealth

About This Book

This book is part of a financial betterment series of "Zero To Hero" publications that are intended to empower individuals by increasing their knowledge of finance, investing, and wealth, so they can achieve a greater level of financial success and enjoy life to the fullest. I believe the information in this series allows individuals to improve not only their own personal lives, but the whole world as well.

This book covers topics that I consider tantamount to ensuring a successful financial future. This book takes an in-depth look at how to build perpetual wealth, the reasons for diversifying your investments, how to approach diversification, and how to leverage different asset classes and diversification strategies to increase your wealth and ensure your personal prosperity.

This book, along with the entire "Zero To Hero" series, is the result of years of research into topics ranging from history and technology to politics, spirituality and finance.

I believe the messages in this book are important for everyone to hear. The topics and strategies I write about in this book are solely my opinions. I am not a financial advisor and you should do your own research before embarking upon a new investment strategy or changing your current strategy. Regardless of whether you agree with my thoughts on things or not, I have always cherished different and new perspectives on topics, and I hope my writings offer you something new to contemplate.

Ethan Galstad
Author

Book Updates and Related Video Content

Supplemental content and videos that go into deeper depth on the topics discussed in this book can be found free of charge on the ZeroToHero website at http://zerotohero.co

Additional resources that correspond to the subjects covered in this book can also be found at the website listed above.

Feedback and Suggestions

Have comments, questions, or suggestions for future revisions of this book or for other ideas you'd like to hear about? I'd love to hear from you!

Contact me on the http://zerotohero.co website and I'll get back to you as soon as I can. Thanks!

About The Author

Some of my fondest memories as a child relate to reading my parents' encyclopedia set. I remember spending hours pulling out each volume and reading about different topics. That love for learning remained a core part of me as I grew up. I loved spending hours at the library perusing different sections and would often spend time on the weekends at used bookstores. Some of my favorite types of books were mysteries, as I was always interested in the discovery of something new or the unearthing of something that was lost or forgotten long ago.

My love of discovering the unknown has led me down a path of attempting to connect the dots between separate viewpoints, topics, and scientific fields throughout my life. This drive to discover something new has led me to create what I consider to be new or different viewpoints and concepts than what others have presented.

About ten years ago I started what is now a multi-million dollar software company. My financial success with that company led me down the path of learning about how to invest my money and build further wealth in what I consider to be a solid investment strategy.

For years I was frustrated by what I felt was the single-focused investment strategy most people had – the stock market. I knew that the truly wealthy of the world didn't just invest in the stock market and I wanted to learn their methodologies for preserving and growing their wealth. That desire let me down an adventure of learning about wealth preservation, risk management, diversification strategies, asset classes, and financial education.

Using the knowledge I gained, I developed my own personal investment and diversification strategy that I have employed for preserving and building my own personal wealth. I believe that others can benefit from what I've learned. Thus, I have taken myself to the task of writing this book. I hope you find it useful in your life.

Regardless of whether you agree with my thoughts on things or not, I have always cherished different and new perspectives on topics, and I hope my writings offer you something new to contemplate.

Foreword

My intention with this book is to help people maximize their financial well-being and prosperity. I have written this book in a manner that presents complex ideas and systems in an easy to understand format, so as to ensure it is received as well as possible by a large, diverse audience. I welcome any feedback, questions, and criticisms you may have on the ideas I present.

As I've stated before, I do not consider myself to be an all-knowing expert in investing or any other given area. I am also not a CPA or certified financial advisor. Rather, I have a broad understanding of a number of different topics, and a good deal of knowledge from my own experience and from the experiences of others.

What I consider to be right for me may not be right for you. I don't know your situation and I don't recommend any specific strategy for your personal finances. Rather, in this book I present ideas that I consider to be solid, that I use on a regular basis, and that I recommend readers investigate for themselves.

I encourage you to not simply accept what I write as outright facts. Rather, I believe it is in your best interest to seek differing opinions on the topics I present, so you can make your own decisions. Remember... a wise man (or woman) seeks the counsel of multiple perspectives before accepting new ideas or adjusting their worldview.

I rarely ever trust one person's opinion (or one book's ideas or philosophies) before making my own decisions. Seek knowledge from different sources and people and make your own decisions and judgments as to what is the best path for you to follow and what ideologies fit with yours. This is your life, so live it without regret and follow your inner voice and gut feeling always. As they say, to thine own self be true.

Thanks to my mentors, role models, and friends who helped inspire and review this book. And thanks to the Amazon team for building an amazing platform that allows independent-minded thinkers to self-publish books in minimal time. Last but not least, thank you for taking some of your precious time to read my books. I truly hope you find them insightful and helpful in your life.

Best regards,

Ethan Galstad
Author

Perpetual Wealth

How to Achieve Financial Freedom and Ensure You Never Run Out of Money

Perpetual Wealth

Table of Contents

Section 1 – Introduction

Introduction 17

Dire Straights 25

Headed Towards The Cliff 27

Opportunity Awaits 43

This Book Can't Help You 45

Section 2 – Core Wealth Concepts

Are You Ready To Be Wealthy? 51

Money And The Root Of Evil 57

The Difference Between The Wealthy And The Poor 61

Pay Yourself First 65

Investing In Yourself 69

Learn From The Best 71

Why Saving Money Won't Make You Rich 77

Trading Your Time And Life For Money 79

Abundance Through Good Money Habits 83

Precursors To Building Wealth 87

Types Of Income 89

Section 3 – Wealth Machine Basics

Why The Rich Don't Work For Money 93

Invest In Assets Not Liabilities 95

Why Cash Flow Is King 101

Never Spend The Principal 103

Allocating Income To Build Wealth 105

Making Your Money Work For You 109

Time Is Of The Essence 111

Class Is In Session 115

Liquid Gold 117

Accredited Advantage 121

The Wealth Machine Blueprint 125

Send Out Your Army 127

Section 4 – Wealth Diversification

The Importance Of Diversification 133

A Strategy For Diversification 135

Asset Allocation 141

Section 5 – Assets For Building And Preserving Wealth

Cash 147

Stocks 155

Lending 163

Real Estate 169

Farmland 175

Precious Metals 179

Cryptocurrency 189

Collectibles 195

Other Alternative Assets 201

Section 6 – Shake Your Money Maker

Generating More Income With High Efficiency 207

Section 7 – Final Thoughts

Final Thoughts 217

Section 8 – Resources

References And Resources 225

Perpetual Wealth

Section 1 - Introduction

Chapter One
Introduction

Disaster. That's what millions of people are currently facing or will soon face in regards to their financial situation. Lives will be ruined and retirement dreams will be shattered. Millions upon millions will find themselves in poverty. Most aren't even aware of the danger that awaits them.

But things don't look that bleak for everyone. For some, their financial future is bright and secure. They have perpetual wealth and will never run out of money in their lifetime.

Why? Because they took charge of their own financial future, sought wise counsel, took action, exercised discipline, and grew their wealth. And their wealth continues to grow without them having to work a 9-to-5 job like the vast majority of people. They've achieved not only financial independence and freedom, but have all but guaranteed that they'll never find themselves wanting for money again.

Your future can be brighter if you choose to make it so. But you can't just want it – you have to learn and take action.

You have to apply discipline. You have to take risks and you have to be prudent. You have to be willing to make mistakes and you have to learn from your mistakes. You have to learn. You have to be willing to break from the herd. You have to follow your own gut instincts. And you need to have the knowledge, tools, and skillset to achieve financial greatness.

That's why I wrote this book. I want you to have as much knowledge as possible to help you achieve your financial goals. I want you to not only achieve financial independence, but financial security, a bountiful retirement, and lasting wealth that can outlive you and your heirs.

The cause of most people's lack of financial security comes down to one main cause – lack of financial education. People don't understand money, wealth, investments, assets, and liabilities. They don't understand risk management, debt, leverage, asset classes, and correlation.

They weren't taught those subjects in school and they don't often learn about them on their own. They only learn the hard way when they run into financial ruin. In reality, most don't even learn a lesson when things go wrong.

People don't generally learn the lesson that's staring them in the face. They don't take corrective action to improve their future. Instead, they just get frustrated and angry from the blow that they never recover from.

They're quick to blame others, but rarely ever take personal responsibility and action to learn and remedy their situation. They're simply victims. Whether they're the victim of the educational system, the banking system, or their own accord is beside the point.

The point is that each of us has to take personal responsibility for our own actions, our thoughts, and our own future. The government isn't going to save us, regardless of what the politicians may say. It's up to each of us to look out for ourselves.

Most people put their financial future in other people's hands. They hand over their hard-earned money to someone else to manage. They place all their trust in the stock market. They place their trust and their financial future in the hands of bankers and corporations that could care less about their success. They put their trust in so-called "experts" who more often than not are just looking to sell them something. They leave themselves open to being screwed in the end.

It's no wonder most people are not informed. It's because they were never taught.

Think about it. When in school were you taught the basics of money, finance, debt, or investing? When were you taught about how to open a checking account or balance your checkbook? When were you taught about wise and unwise use of credit and debt? When were you taught about taxes, getting a mortgage on a house, or how to invest your money? You weren't.

Robert Kiyosaki, author of "Rich Dad Poor Dad" and several other best-selling books, calls this lack of financial education the "conspiracy of the rich". I would have to agree with him. It almost seems as though the lack of financial education in the world is intentional.

Instead of learning the basic life-long skills of money and finance, students are forced to learn English literature. Instead of learning how to make wise investments, they're forced to take band class or sing in choir. Instead of learning how to get a mortgage or pay taxes, they're forced to take biology and sociology.

The fact is, very few people will ever make use of biology, sociology, band, English literature, or most of what they learn in school in their post-school years. Those things generally don't contribute too much in the course of their careers and long-term future.

Money, finance, debt, and taxes, however, are things that matter in a big way to each and every member of society. So why aren't we taught these things in middle school, high school, or college? Think about that. It's messed up.

What are people taught about saving for retirement? Most people only know what the "experts" and their friends and colleagues tell them. Invest in a "well-balanced" portfolio of stocks, bonds, and mutual funds through a 401k or IRA ad save for the long term.

The sad reality is that most people don't know much of anything about how to really ensure a financially secure retirement. They know very little about investing. They know almost nothing about alternative investments. They think diversification is keeping all their eggs in the same basket. If all they have is a 401k or IRA, they're not really diversified.

The purpose of this book is to open your eyes to what I consider a better way of ensuring a strong financial future. It's a book about how to manage risk, how to approach diversification, how to invest in multiple asset classes, how to develop passive income streams, and how to help ensure your long-term financial success.

It's a book that I believe is worth its weight in gold if you apply the principles outlined in the following chapters.

I believe many people are headed towards financial doom in their retirement years. I feel terrible for them and I want to help you avoid the pitfalls they will likely face in their future. I want you to be prosperous and wealthy enough to make not only your retirement better, but allow you to leave something behind to your heirs.

In this book I will cover several topics that will hopefully open your eyes to the problems and challenges we face, the opportunities that are available, and courses of action that can help protect you and enrich you financially.

While this book offers both strategy and specific actions you can take to increase your wealth, you'll find that I spend a good deal of this book talking about mindset. The reason for that is that mindset is the biggest determining factor as to whether someone will succeed or fail. If you do not have the right mindset you will not reach great levels of success. You must be willing to learn new things, unlearn old ways of thinking, and have the audacity to be great if you want to achieve greatness.

As I stated earlier, I encourage you to not simply accept what I write as outright facts. Rather, I believe it is in your best interest to seek differing opinions on the topics I present, so you can make your own decisions.

Remember… a wise man (or woman) seeks the counsel of multiple perspectives before accepting new ideas or adjusting their worldview. I rarely ever trust one person's opinion (or one book's ideas or philosophies) before making my own decisions.

Seek knowledge from different sources and people and make your own decisions and judgments as to what is the best path for you to follow and what ideologies fit with yours.

This is your life, so live it without regret and follow your inner voice and gut feeling always. As they say, to thine own self be true.

FYI, you will find that I often refer to the "poor", "rich" and "wealthy" in this book. The term "poor" is not meant to demean anyone. I, myself, have been poor. I have simply taken the lead of other authors who have used to term to reference anyone (including the middle class and affluent) that are not wealthy, regardless of their material possessions or the size of their bank account. The term "rich", as I use it, often refers to people that have money, but who are not necessarily wealthy. The term "wealthy" refers to those who achieved true financial freedom, along with all the riches it provides.

I have been poor and have changed my life and financial situation to where I am now wealthy. I have done this through hard work, continuous learning, and action. I hope to share what I've learned to help you improve your financial situation and become wealthy at a faster pace than I have.

Perpetual Wealth

Chapter Two

Dire Straights

The world we live in seems to be more fragile than ever. The economy looks to be headed for another recession, the stock market looks due for a major correction (aka "crash"), the easy money policy of the Federal Reserve means our money is becoming more worthless day by day, and the growing national debt spells doom in the not too distant future.

We're living in a time in the United States where there is a growing gap between the rich and the poor. This gap has led to unprecedented – at least in recent history – discontent, protest, and political outrage. A battle between the haves and the have nots threatens the stability of our society. As the gap grows larger, so does the danger of discontent.

To add to the national crisis that we seem to be hurtling towards, the personal financial situation of the vast majority of the population is pretty dire as well. People are burdened with credit card debt and student loans that they can't afford. They're spending more than they make, living on easy credit, and failing to save and invest for their future.

People's retirement dreams are being ruined. They're having to work well into their 70's or beyond. Many are unable to recover from unexpected job losses or downsizing. Their jobs are being outsourced overseas and they're being displaced by younger workers, automation, and artificial intelligence.

Their savings is either non-existent or insufficient to support their lifestyle. Their retirement accounts are either woefully underfunded or incapable of providing for the dreams they had. The promises of pensions that could provide for a secure retirement are either faltering or non-existent.

Stock market crashes threaten to wipe out 401ks and IRAs. Hackers and cybercriminals can wipe out bank accounts and financial holdings in a fraction of a second. Identity thieves lie waiting, willing and eager to steal your hard-earned wealth and lay claim to your assets.

The national debt continues to grow, while the government continues to print money to keep our economic system afloat. Saving money now means losing purchasing power due to inflation.

For many people, their financial future looks pretty bleak. Disastrous really. And most aren't even aware of what awaits them.

For the wealthy, however, the story is different. Their future is secure, their riches continue to grow, and they will escape the financial doom that many others face. The purpose of this book is to help you secure your wealth so that you may prosper in the future, rather than be a victim of financial doom.

Chapter Three

Headed Towards The Cliff

I find myself being constantly surprised and disappointed when I hear about people's financial situation. The term "situation" doesn't really fit. "Disaster" is more appropriate a term for what most people have when it comes to their financial well-being.

The reports and figures that come out of news organizations, think tanks, and polling groups are absolutely miserable.

40% HAVE LESS THAN $400 IN EMERGENCY SAVINGS

The Personal Savings Crisis

Nearly half – yes HALF - of all Americans don't have even $400 saved for an emergency. Additionally, nearly 70% of Americans have less than $1,000 saved. That means that only 30% of the population has $1,000 or more saved. That is absolutely crazy!

There is no good reason why those percentages should be so high. None whatsoever. It only takes setting aside less than

$20 per week for just a year to develop a $1,000 savings fund for emergencies.

People would much rather spends hundreds per month on their cellphones, cable, Internet, movies, take-out, and lattes than exercise a minimal amount of restraint to build up a basic emergency fund.

Nearly 80% of Americans say they're living paycheck-to-paycheck. That means all but a small minority of people are spending all (or more than) they bring in for income each month.

80% LIVE PAYCHECK TO PAYCHECK

You'll hear the reason for this is that their jobs just don't pay them well enough. The fact is that most people simply don't exercise self-control. They don't live within their means. They want more than they can afford and they spend more than they make to get the things they want now. That kind of out-of-control spending will be their financial doom.

CREDIT CARD DEBT PER HOUSEHOLD: $6,000

When their income isn't enough to support their spending habits, people often turn to credit cards. Recent studies have shown that the average household in America has approximately $6,000 in credit card debt. With most credit cards sporting hefty interest rates, that makes for some substantial additional costs for the things that people buy - most of which doesn't have much of any real long-lasting value.

People often don't think about the future when they overspend and fail to save and invest for their future. They prefer to focus on the here and now, rather than thinking about what the years ahead might hold for them. This can hurt them tremendously when retirement nears.

Tragically, most people don't put away enough financial security to ensure they'll have the easy retirement they've been dreaming of.

A 2018 report from the TransAmerica Center For Retirement Studies contained many disturbing financial statistics regarding retirees, including these:

- **40%** of retirees are **still paying off debt** - either credit card or mortgage debt
- **Social security** (not savings or investments) is the **primary source** (oftentimes the only) of income for most retirees
- **Over a third** of retirees say their financial situation has **deteriorated** since retiring

Entering retirement while still owing on a mortgage, credit card debt, or student loans is tantamount to committing financial suicide – especially if you're relying on Social Security as your primary source of income.

The average monthly Social Security check as of January 2019 was just **$1,461**. That equates to around just **$17,500 per year**. Paying off debt and the covering the basic expenses of life are going to take a large chunk out of that. Forget living the high life that you've dreamed of if Social Security is all that you have to rely on in your golden years.

If you end up relying solely on Social Security when you retire, there's a better chance than not that you will be living close to the poverty line. That's no way to spend your golden years, in my opinion.

The Retirement Account Crisis

Most people have been indoctrinated to put their retirement savings in 401ks and IRAs. The average amount that people about to enter retirement have in their 401ks is startling low.

Vanguard's "How America Saves 2019" report concluded that the average American 65 years or older had about **$193,000** in their 401k, with the median balance being around **$58,000**. Neither the average nor the median balances are likely to offer much financial security in retirement.

An October 2017 report by the Government Accountability Office (GAO) concluded that the median retirement savings for Americans ages 55-64 was **$107,000**. According to the GAO, that amount would only equate to a **$310/month** payment if put into an inflation-adjusted annuity. $310 a month doesn't go far to pay the bills, cover medical costs, or put food on the table.

The Pension Crisis

Unless you work in government, or are a baby boomer, the concept of having a pension is probably a foreign one. And if you don't have one currently, you're not likely to get one of the future.

Pension plans are considered defined benefit (DB) plans. Defined benefit plans provide a retiree with a steady, fixed amount of income on a regular basis (usually monthly). The amount of a person's benefit (payment) is often defined by their number of years of service in a company or organization.

In 1974 the rules of retirement and retirement plans changed. The Employee Retirement Income Security Act (ERISA) that was enacted in 1974 placed increased requirements on companies that offered pension plans and left them liable if things went wrong. This, like many other government regulations, would end up having a negative effect on the middle class.

After congress passed the Revenue Act of 1978, they opened the way to the 401k. In essence, the government incentivized companies to stop offering pension plans and start pushing employees to 401k plans. The availability of the 401k allowed companies to stop offering defined benefit (DB) plans and transitioned employees to defined contribution (DC) plans.

Defined contribution plans are retirement plans where it is the individual's sole responsibility to contribute to the plan. The amount of retirement funds available to a retiree is dependent on what they saved during their working years.

Recent statistics from Fidelity show that individuals aged 60-69 have an average of about **$195,000** in their 401k. If you were to adopt the rule of 4% for withdrawing on an average 401k balance, you'd be able to take out about **$650/month.**

That figure assumes that the stock market is performing well. If the stock market experiences a correction of 30%, not only would the 401k balance decrease, but the monthly withdrawal rate would have to drop to around **$450/month**.

According to many experts, 401ks are extremely underfunded and place retirees at risk of financial insecurity. A full-blown retirement crisis is underway, and it's not just limited to 401ks.

Even if you pay attention the news, you'll likely miss the rarely mentioned issues related to the solvency of pension accounts. If you dig deep on Google and YouTube, you'll find some startling news - pensions are facing tough times.

Many municipalities are facing a pension problem – underfunded liabilities. What that means in a nutshell is that pension plans don't have enough money to pay out the promised amounts to retirees. They've overpromised and now are facing the problems of the shortfalls in their pension funds. Some are ignoring the problems and kicking the can down the road, while others are making drastic changes that negatively affect pensioners.

In some cases pension payments are being cut by as much as **60%**. That type of cut can prove disastrous to those already in retirement, or those about to retire. When you're counting on receiving a certain amount each month, it can severely affect your retirement plans.

Looking at the decisions and actions of those in government and those managing pension funds, I'd say the road is going to get even tougher in the years ahead. If you've been promised a pension and are relying on receiving a full pension in your retirement years, I'd advise you to start making backup plans immediately.

If you don't believe me, just do some research on Google and YouTube. If you have eyes to see and ears to hear, you can't deny what's started to happen.

Case in point, as I'm writing this book, a new article from wirepoints.com just appeared that outlines the city of Chicago's unfolding pension crisis. According to the article (a link is found in the resource section at the end of this book) Chicago's city and school pension funds are **underfunded by $70 billion**. To put that into perspective, if the population of Chicago were to have to cover that shortfall (which they likely will in the form of higher taxes), this shortfall equates to a debt of over **$143,000 per household**. That's an incredible level of debt obligation for each Chicago resident. And it's only bound to get worse in the coming years.

When it comes to retirement (and many other matters in my opinion), the promises of politicians are clearly worthless. As time goes by, they seem to be primarily focused on getting re-elected, which in turn allows debt to grow, pensions to get depleted, and people's dreams to be shattered.

Buyer Beware

If you leave your financial future to others, you're likely to suffer. If you believe the promises of government, Wall Street, or most of the financial advisors out there, you're likely to be not only disappointed, but left feeling betrayed and powerless.

The fact is, you must take control of your financial future yourself. You have to take responsibility, and you have to take action. If you let others take the wheel of your financial future, your ultimate destination isn't really in your sphere of control.

That doesn't mean you shouldn't consult with financial advisors. It just means that you should consider that they might not have all the right answers. Your future is ultimately in your own hands and blaming your financial advisors when you run our of money in your senior years isn't going to do a whole lot of good.

We're all indoctrinated with what we "should" and "shouldn't" do. We're told how we should save for retirement, how we should invest, and how we should save. We are rarely ever taught the larger systems of money, finance, and investing. We aren't taught about good debt vs. bad debt. We aren't taught about how to pay our taxes, how to balance a checkbook, how to master the basics of money and investing. We're all basically left to fend for ourselves and to figure things out along the way.

I don't put much faith or trust in others when it comes to my financial future. I put even less trust in the government. It's not that I'm paranoid. It's because I'm skeptical at best, and an unbeliever at worst. It's because I've learned more from my research and experience than I've heard anywhere from government or the so-called experts. I've learned to do my own research, learned to take action, and learned what does and doesn't work in my own financial life.

Working Into Old Age

The sad reality is that many retirees will be forced to continue working past their ideal retirement age because they lack the financial stability to stop working. This, of course, assumes that jobs will be available to them if they need to seek employment.

If there are more people of retirement age looking for a job than there are jobs available, there's not much hope for finding employment. You don't want to find yourself in this situation. In fact, I don't think you want to have to continue working into your golden years. If you're financially secure and want to get back to work of your own free will, that's another matter entirely.

It's Not Looking Good

Based on the data that's available, I'd say that most Americans are in serious financial trouble when it comes to retirement. Failing to save and invest properly through their lifetime is going to cause an enormous amount of pain in their golden years. I feel absolutely terrible for them.

I'm doing my best to make sure I'm in a solid financial place for my retirement and I want to help you do the same. I don't want you to suffer from lack of financial security like millions are likely to.

Beyond the savings, investment, and pension crises that are just beginning to unfold, there are several other cautionary indicators that provide a warning about what is likely in store for the greater economy.

Most people will scoff at the idea of an economic downturn when things are seemingly going well. They have the mentality of "things are different this time", as if things being different is going to hold back the tide of the storm. They think "it won't happen again" or "the economy is strong". When they think like this and fail to see the potential problems that could lie ahead, they're caught up in a mixture of irrational exuberance and normalcy bias.

Irrational exuberance is an enthusiast and positive outlook that is unfounded based on the underlying fundamentals, statistics, and data that are available. Instead of being based on facts, a person's viewpoint is fueled by emotion.

Normalcy bias is a person's inability to believe that things could be wrong or that problems are around the corner. Why? Because the present situation (e.g. a strong economy) is what they know – it's their "normal". People who suffer from normalcy bias tend to not do well when a "new normal" arrives as the result of a calamity of some kind.

To be successful in building and keeping your wealth, you must avoid the pitfalls of irrational exuberance and normalcy bias. You have to be willing to look past the current situation and see what might be coming around the corner. You have to do this so that you can position yourself and your wealth to ride out potential storms and be ready to capitalize on opportunities when everyone else is running around scared straight.

When the next economic storm arrives, it is likely to cause a tsunami of trouble for existing retirees, soon-to-be retirees, and those that have been saving and investing for retirement.

A Looming Recession

As of mid 2019, there are a number of indicators that the economy is about to enter a recession. As this book is not focused on the general economy, I won't go into detail on them, save for one that people are generally familiar with – the unemployment rate.

Most people hold the belief that low unemployment rates indicate that the economy is strong. For the most part, they are correct.

However, contrary to popular belief, low unemployment rates aren't always a good sign. The chart below shows historical unemployment rates, along with periods of economic recession (indicated by shaded sections) from 1948 to mid-2019.

Perpetual Wealth

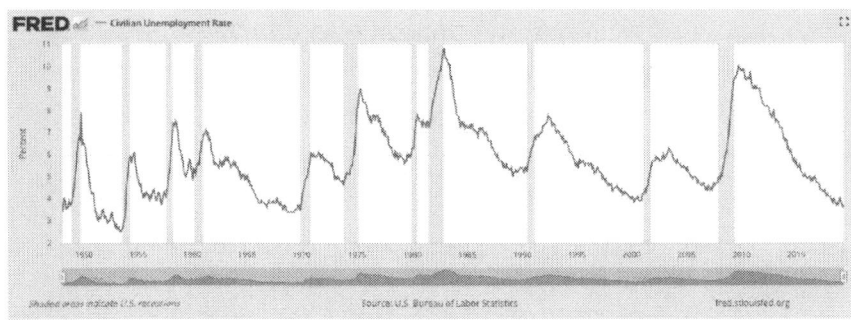

Image Source: U.S. Bureau of Labor Statistics, Civilian Unemployment Rate [UNRATE], retrieved from FRED, Federal Reserve Bank of St. Louis; https://fred.stlouisfed.org/series/UNRATE , July 2, 2019.

As you can see in the chart, low unemployment rates correspond to the start of a recession. Once a recession starts, unemployment rates spike.

Recessions have a history of causing an enormous amount of damage to the financial security and well being of millions of people.

During the so-called "Great Recession" of 2007-2009, household net worth dropped by approximately 18%, 30 million people lost their jobs, and long-term unemployment doubled it's previous historical highs.

During the Great Recession many people who became unemployed were unable to find another job for nearly a year. Many older workers were unable to find a job and were forced into early retirement.

The long-term unemployment figures were so startling, that many financial experts recommended that people develop emergency savings funds that could support basic living expenses for at least 9-12 months. That was an increase over previous suggestions that people have an emergency fund to cover 3 months of living expenses.

Fake Money And The Everything Bubble

In 1971 President Nixon took the United States off the gold standard. Prior to that fateful year, each US dollar was backed by gold – an asset that has proven a stable store of value since ancient times. Once the US dollar was taken off the gold standard, it became what we call a "fiat" (fake) currency.

Fiat currency is simply money that we believe has value because someone (e.g. the government) tells us it does. It is essentially fake money because there's no real store of value behind it.

The danger in fiat currencies is that every fiat currency in history has always fallen in value to zero. The reason for this is that governments have the ability to print or create money out of thin air whenever they want.

When governments print or create money without any real store of value that backs that money, it creates an artificial environment where inflation or hyperinflation can take over and destroy the purchasing power of the currency. It also allows investors and speculators to purchase additional assets (e.g. stocks and real estate). The purchasing of these assets can lead to pricing bubbles where the supposed value of said assets exceed their actual value. This can have disastrous consequences when the economy enters a recession or experiences a crash.

In an effort to help end the Great Recession, the Federal Reserve printed money out of thin air in an attempt to stabilize the economy. This process was referred to as "Quantitative Easing" (QE). That sounds like a technical economic term, but all it really means is that the US dollar supply increased dramatically because money was created magically out of thin air.

This increase in the money supply allowed the economy to recover quicker because it opened up the credit market, which allowed banks to offer credit to customers. The re-opening of easy money (credit) has allowed speculators to artificially increase the price of assets like the stock market and real estate.

Many experts – including Jim Rickards and Mike Maloney – believe that the increase in the fiat money supply will have drastic, long-lasting consequences for our financial system and economy. Namely, they believe a period of deflation followed by hyperinflation will occur, followed by a rebalancing of the value of gold – potentially to $15,000 or more per oz of gold. This would represent an increase in the value of gold by more than 1,000% and is not so much an indicator of the worth of gold as it would be a show of the relative worthlessness of the US dollar.

Because the government can print money out of thin air, our country is always going to be able to pay our obligations (e.g. debts). But ensuring the purchasing power of the US dollar (e.g. what you can buy with your dollars) cannot be guaranteed. Thus, relying on the number of dollars in your nest egg isn't a great method of ensuring your future wealth and prosperity.

There are several ways to avoid the catastrophic consequences of hyperinflation and I'll cover these later in this book. Protecting your wealth is just as important as growing your wealth, so it's important to hedge against economic turmoil and fiat currency.

Let It Be

There are plenty of other danger signs in the global economy right now, but I'll spare you the details for the time being.

There are so many evident problems on the horizon that it's best to focus on how to avoid those problems and secure your wealth instead of focusing on the potential downsides to the overall economy.

After all, there's no point in talking about our sinking ship. Let's get started on building life rafts to ensure we survive the coming turbulent economic waters and achieve perpetual wealth.

Perpetual Wealth

Chapter Four
Opportunity Awaits

If you're read to this point, you're probably thinking this book is full of gloom and doom. Rest assured, it isn't. Most people don't want to look at the negative side of things, and that can hurt them in the long run.

To truly understand money and build wealth over time, it is critical that you understand the ups and downs of the economy and financial system, how others use or misuse money, and how you can leverage your money to build lasting wealth.

As you progress through this book you'll find information that can provide you with the tools necessary to succeed financially.

A key component of that process is starting with an understanding of where we as a society stand in regards to financial stability. Another is to understand how your mindset affects your ability to create and keep wealth.

Other key aspects are understanding what true assets really are, what types of asset classes exist, and how to go about structuring your investments in a way that provides lasting wealth.

With the knowledge in this book, you can create "wealth machines" that provide perpetual wealth and ensure that you never run out of money.

By building wealth machines, you can get to a point where your money is working for you, rather than you having to work for money. Once your wealth machines bring in more money than you spend, you have achieved the ultimate definition of financial freedom.

With the knowledge of assets classes that this book provides, you can set yourself up to survive financial and economic storms with your wealth preserved.

This is what I want to help you do. I want you to succeed financially, become truly wealthy, and achieve financial freedom.

I hope you find the information in the book useful in your life. If you do, please share your knowledge with others, so that they may succeed as well.

Chapter Five
This Book Can't Help You

I want you to be wealthy, to have a secure retirement, to be financially free, and to be able to pass something to your heirs. I believe the information, principles, and suggestions in this book can help you achieve those things.

I have written this book in a manner that I hope can be easily understood by many people. I have attempted to explain complex topics in a simple, easy to understand manner. I have done this with the goal of making the process of building and keeping wealth within the reach of whomever reads this book.

Despite my best intentions and my greatest wishes for your success, I know for certain that this book cannot help you if these apply to you:

- **You live beyond your means.** Money, finance, and wealth are principled in mathematics. There is no mathematical formula that works for building and keeping wealth if you spend more than you earn. You must live below you means to make wise use of your money and build your wealth.

- **You never question what you're told**. If you can't step out of the mindset that your only way to a secure and stable retirement is to put all your investments in the stock market, the information in this book will be useless to you. You must be able to think for yourself and make your own decisions – free of the mental slavery we are all indoctrinated with – if you are to achieve lasting wealth.

- **You're not disciplined.** Investing your money wisely requires that you exercise discipline in how you spend, save, and invest your money. If you do not have self-control or you lack the discipline to develop and stick to a plan, this book cannot help you.

- **You believe that money is the root of all evil.** If you believe this lie to be true, you are creating a block to your financial success. You must understand that money is good if you want to accumulate wealth. After all, why would your subconscious allow you to obtain something you think is evil?

- **You believe the wealthy are bad people**. If you have a poor view of wealthy people, and yet at the same time are working on trying to become wealthy yourself, you are blocking your path to success. Remember, you become what you think. If you think poorly of wealthy people you will likely never achieve great wealth. A poor mindset equates to being poor. Appreciate the wealthy, learn all you can about how they made and kept their money, and apply the principles from their success roadmap to your life and you stand to succeed far more than others who do not. You must think like the rich to become rich.

- **You're not willing to learn**. In order to become wealthy, you are going to have to learn about investments, finance, and how the wealthy think and act. If you're not willing to learn, you're going to miss out on opportunities and you're likely to lose a lot of money by making ill-informed decisions.

- **You're not willing to fail or take risks**. Everything in life has risk. You're going to have to take calculated risks on your path to building wealth. Sometimes things are going to fail and sometimes you're going to lose money. You have to be willing to take a risk and be willing to lose money if you want to build true wealth. As they say, there is no reward without the risk.

- **You procrastinate**. Time is of the essence when building wealth. Time can work for you or against you when it comes to compounded interest, re-invested dividends, and opportunities. If you fail to act, someone else will and you'll lose out on the opportunity. You're going to lose out if you procrastinate, delay decision-making, or fail to act in a timely manner.

- **You're not willing to put in the time.** There's no magic fairy that is going to do your work for you. If you want to invest well, become wealthy, and have a secure financial future, you must be proactive and make it happen. This requires work. Work requires time. If you don't make the time, you won't make it to the finish line.

- **You are not patient**. Achieving great wealth and financial prosperity doesn't happen overnight. What you need on your side is time. Time is limited, so delays in taking action to building wealth cost you dearly. Once you do start, time is required for your wealth to multiply and grow. You can always make more money, but you can never make more time, so use the time you have wisely and be patient with the process.

- **You think you have enough money already**. If you've saved a substantial amount of money or sold your business and received a lump sump and are happy with what you have, you're missing the point of building wealth. When you have set amount of money – no matter how large – you have a finite supply of money. To build true wealth, you must put your money to work to generate additional money and ensure you never run out. This is one of the critical things that people who win the lottery or receive a large sum of money through inheritance or a business sale fail to realize. That's why so many run out of money and eventually declare bankruptcy.

If you don't suffer from these blocks to lasting wealth, you're on the right track! If you do, do your best to address them. If you can't, you can stop reading here. I don't want you to waste your time reading the rest of this book, as it won't do you much good. Time is precious, so spend it doing what's right for you!

Section 2

-

Core Wealth Concepts

Perpetual Wealth

Chapter Six

Are You Ready To Be Wealthy?

Everyone wants to have more money. Everyone wants more wealth. But not everyone is ready and able to obtain and achieve more. In order to achieve financial wealth, you have to be ready for it. You have to make sure you're prepared for it before you can effectively achieve it. Here are a few things that I think are important requirements to getting ready to become wealthy.

Discipline Required

Building and keeping wealth requires a great deal of discipline. It's not a "set it and forget it" thing. It's going to require your attention and active participation all along the way, and it's going to require continuous learning and evaluation. The path to obtaining true and lasting wealth is not a spectator sport.

Frankly, very few people have the discipline required to accomplish large goals in life. They simply give up too easily, get distracted by other things, or make excuses about why they can't do something.

If you like to make excuses or can't apply yourself faithfully to an endeavor, you don't have a wealthy mindset and you're not likely to obtain true wealth.

Money Might Change You

Some people say that money changes you. That's somewhat true, but not in a bad way. In truth, money doesn't change who you are. Instead, it simply amplifies who you already are.

For example, if you like buying shoes before you become wealthy, you're likely to buy even more shoes when you're wealthy. If you're a good person before you come into money, you'll be a good person after you have money.

One thing that wealth will change in you is your ability to relax knowing that your financial future is secure. It will provide you with the things and experiences that can enrich your life. It will increase your happiness (to a point) by providing you with those things.

Having more money will (hopefully) let you appreciate life far more than those who simply work their years away by chasing their next paycheck. Once you're truly wealthy you won't need to trade your time for money. Instead, your money will be working for you. And that will allow you the freedom to spend your time doing the things in life that really matter to you.

You Might Lose Friends

You generally won't find successful people talking about this topic much. Most people don't understand what it takes to become successful and what you have to do to get there. They'll focus on the outcome, while ignoring the path that successful people had to take to achieve their wealth.

From my own experience as an entrepreneur, I went through stages where I lost friends and acquaintances due to my success. Some of the people who supported me when I was getting started became jealous and critical once I became successful.

I've talked with several other successful entrepreneurs who have experienced the same thing in their own lives. And you'll likely experience it when you become more successful too.

I believe the basic reason why this happens is envy. Everyone loves an underdog and the story of someone who's going through a struggle. But once a hero emerges, they grow envious of the fame and/or fortune that person achieves.

You shouldn't fear losing friends are your success grows. You'll find new friends and acquaintances that better align with your successful self than your old circle. That's a good thing, because your circle of friends and influencers determines your future success. If you surround yourself with good, positive people that challenge you, have high aspirations and a good work ethic, you're much more likely to succeed than if you have people around you that don't exemplify those attributes.

Overcoming Blocks To Wealth

In order to become wealthy, you're first going to have to free yourself of any blocks to wealth that might be holding you back. Without even knowing it, most of us have negative views of money and wealth pounded into our subconscious from a young age.

Before you can be effective at building your wealth, you have to examine why you want the wealth, how you're going to build it, and what obstacles might block your path in achieving it.

Let's examine some of the wealth blocks that society tries to ingrain in us...

Money Isn't All That Matters

No kidding. People that say this are often the one's who don't have as much money as they need or would like to have. It's almost used as an excuse as to why they don't have the financial resources they'd like.

It's true that your experiences and relationships in life are more important than money itself. However, money helps you have more wonderful experiences, improve your standard of living, and provide for your family. And those things do matter.

What's a valuable lesson to learn is that money doesn't matter until it does. If you or a family member are faced with a disease that could be solved by an expensive surgery, money <u>will</u> matter. If you have the money, you can have the life-saving surgery. If you don't have money, you can't. Money does matter. Big time.

Money Doesn't Bring Happiness

This saying is also parroted by people that don't have as much money as they'd like. This is partially true, but not in the context or manner that people use it in. The truth is that a lack of money can severely affect your happiness in life. If you don't have enough money, you can find yourself stressed through life. And that will make you unhappy.

It is true that an increase in your wealth doesn't correspond directly to your happiness. A millionaire isn't a million times happier than the person that has one dollar to their name. There is certainly a diminishing return with regards to how much happiness money can buy.

Money Doesn't Make You A Bad Person

When I was a teenager, there were a few rich kids in my school. Actually, the kids weren't rich. They were the kids of rich parents. And some of those kids were mean (or at least I thought they were). That impression led me to create a construct in my mind that equated having money to being a bad person. I had to address that issue and see that it wasn't true before I could become financially successful.

In society today, there is a growing discontent over the wealth gap. People refer to this as "wealth inequality", as if all people are supposed to share wealth equally. I for one do not feel obligated to give my wealth to those who have chosen not to save, invest, or grow their own wealth. Nor do I think it right that the government, or anyone else for that matter, should have the right to forcefully take it from me to give to others.

Still, many people hold the view that the "1 percent" in society are somehow evil and should be made to pay for everything the 99 percent want. Calls to tax the rich are heard loudly in political rallies. The rich are made out to be evil people who have taken advantage of others in order to have accumulated their wealth. Socialist ideals seem to be spreading like wildfire.

I know many people who despise the rich. And yet I don't know a single person – not a single one – who would not like to be a millionaire or multi-millionaire themselves. That's real hypocrisy in action. If you hold a negative view of wealthy people, what do you think the chances are that you will yourself become wealthy?

Money Is The Root Of All Evil

Societal beliefs about money can be strange and even downright lies. The mantra that "money is the root of all evil" is something that I believe holds people back in achieving great wealth. Since this is a pretty pervasive and damaging lie that we've all been told, I'll examine (and destroy) it in the next chapter.

Chapter Seven

Money And The Root Of Evil

We've all hard the saying "Money is the root of all evil". It's been repeated several times in our lives. I don't believe this statement to be true at all. In fact, I believe this to be an outright lie. I believe the opposite – that **the lack of money is the root of much evil**.

From my viewpoint, it's almost as if society is working against the population achieving financial freedom and great wealth with negative money mantras.

I'm a firm believer that your belief systems and mindset impact your destiny. If you believe money is bad, or that people with money are bad, you're sabotaging your chances of becoming wealthy. Belief systems that are in our subconscious can negatively affect us even more effectively than conscious thoughts.

I don't like lies – especially big lies that negatively affect millions of people. Thus, I'll break down the system of money, examine it from every angle, and show you that money isn't evil. I'll show you how money is good everywhere you look and why you should want more of it in your life.

When you earn money from a job, you are providing for yourself and your family. That's good.

When you spend money on the stuff of life (food, clothes, cars, vacations, etc), you're improving your standard of living. That's good. In the process of buying things, you're also helping to support businesses that make and provide those things. You're making the business owners happy. That's good. The businesses can hire employees and provide more paying jobs that help their families. That's good.

When you save money you're making dreams come true. When you deposit $100 in the bank, you're saving for your future. That's good. Additionally, when you deposit that $100, the bank magically creates (through the process of fractional reserve banking) $900 from thin air. The bank then uses that $900 to provide loans to people wanting to buy a home, buy a car, and refinance their debt. When you park money in the bank, you're helping to make dreams come true. That's good.

When you donate money to non-profits, you're helping them help others. That's good.

When you give money to others or cover their tabs, you're making them happy and helping them out. That's good.

When you lend money to others, you're helping cover their expenses and making them happy. That's good. When you get your money back, that's even better.

When you invest money in companies, stocks, and other investments, you're working towards your financial goals. That's good. In the process, you're also providing capital (money) to companies that produce goods and services that improve the world. Those companies in turn employee people, which helps provide a living for many families. That's good.

When you pay taxes, you're helping to do good. Despite the government's inefficiencies and (in my opinion) high tax rates, they do manage to do some good. Your tax dollars help to support education, build and maintain infrastructure, provide for the national defense, and help those on the lower end of the economic spectrum. So that's good too.

I don't see a single area where money is bad. At worst, I see inefficiencies in government. But other than that, it's all good.

So "money is the root of all evil" is a complete lie. I guess the only way money could be bad is if you use it to do bad things. But in that case, it's not the money that's bad – it's you.

The lie of "money is the root of all evil" is a perfect example of why I would caution you to not just outright believe what society and others say. I would challenge you to examine other things you've been told and destroy those lies in your own life. I have no doubt you'll find plenty.

Perpetual Wealth

Chapter Eight
The Difference Between The Wealthy And The Poor

Money isn't the only thing that's different between the wealthy and the poor. There are a number of factors that determine one's wealth (or one's lack thereof) that people often overlook.

When most people think of wealth, they think of it as having the ability to able to have an expensive house, an expensive car, expensive clothes, and expensive vacations. That's not what wealth is. Those are things that can be acquired with money, but those are not what wealth is.

Most people want to look like they're rich, when the reality is that they aren't. If you dig deeper into what most people call "wealth" in most of the country, you'll find it to be a façade. Most people that appear to be rich are actually in debt up to their eyeballs. They look like they're rich, but they're not. They're actually debt slaves to ever-increasing expenses. They're actually poor, even though they look rich.

There's a distinction between being rich and being wealthy that is important to cover. Being rich means that you have money. Being wealthy means that you have flows of money coming into you. That's an important distinction to make that is often lost on people. Whether or not you understand that difference will determine your level of financial success in your lifetime. We'll dive into more on that in the following chapters.

If you want to be truly wealthy, you need to understand some important differences between the wealthy and the poor (including the "fake" rich people who are actually poor). Here are some of the key differences between the wealthy and the poor:

- **The wealthy have a different mindset** than the poor. Instead of thinking "I can't afford that", they think "how could I afford that?" The poor have a poor mindset, while the wealthy have a wealthy mindset.

- **The wealthy have financial education**, whereas the poor do not. Our school systems don't teach kids about money, and as a result they don't understand it in adulthood. The wealthy make it a priority to learn about money, finance, and investments. The poor prioritize their effort on spending, rather than learning.

- **The wealthy understand it's not how much you earn**, but how much you have left to invest. The poor spend all the money they bring in and have nothing left to save or invest.

- **The wealthy pay themselves first**, while the poor pay themselves last. Prioritizing investments improve the financial situation of the wealthy, while the spending habits of the poor keep them slaves to their jobs and their debts.

- **The wealthy buy assets**, while the poor buy liabilities. The wealthy understand that their house is not an asset and they understand the value of buying assets over liabilities. The poor focus their attention on buying liabilities like a new car, a bigger house, etc.

- **The wealthy work on building cash flow streams** to increase their wealth. The poor waste their money on useless shiny doodads.

- **The wealthy focus on continuously building their wealth**, while the poor focus on continuously spending their money.

- **The wealthy make their money work for them**. The poor work for money.

- **The wealthy don't purchase shiny doodads**. Instead, their assets and the cash flow from their assets do. The poor buy shiny doodads with their money.

- **The wealthy take responsibility**, while the poor blame others.

- **The wealthy take action**, while the poor make excuses.

- **The wealthy learn from failure**, while the poor give up after failing.

- **The wealthy take calculated risks**, while the poor are afraid of taking risks.

Being wealthy is much more than simply having money. It's about having the right mindset, the right education, and the discipline to apply yourself to take the actions required to build and keep wealth. Of all of these items, I believe financial education to be of the utmost importance. Without financial education you cannot truly succeed financially. With financial education, the world opens up to you and you can become wealthy.

Robert Kiyosaki – author of the best-selling book *Rich Dad Poor Dad* – called the lack of financial education in our school system the "conspiracy of the rich". I agree wholeheartedly with him. Why don't our schools teach kids about money, finance, and investing?

If you want to become wealthy, you need to make it a priority to educate yourself. Learn from the wealthy. Learn from those who have succeeded. Don't make the mistake of learning from your peers and others who are poor, or you will sabotage your efforts in achieving lasting wealth.

Chapter Nine
Pay Yourself First

A critical mistake that most people make in their finances is to not pay themselves first. This is a critical difference between those who have money and those who do not.

When most people get paid, they pay their bills first (mortgage, rent, utilities, etc) and then spend the rest of what they make on things they don't really need – electronics, vacations, clothing, etc.

We're living in a materialistic society that's increasingly driven by social media and one-upping others. People seem to be caught up in a continuous cycle of trying to look like they have a fabulous life that's full of rich experiences and expensive possessions.

People spend all of their money and go into debt to make it look like they're wealthy, when in fact they are not. Many people are in debt up to their eyeballs. And for what purpose? To feel good about themselves? To make others think more highly of them? These types of poor spending habits will be their downfall in the later stages of life, when they have no financial wealth to support themselves.

Having new experiences and having material things is part of the enjoyment of life. However, it should not be a goal that we pursue at the expense of the future.

While it's true that we all need certain things in life (like clothes), the overall tendency that people have is to spend much more than they have to on items that don't contribute to their wealth.

The wealthy (and those on their way to becoming wealthy) take a different approach.

Wealthy people set aside enough money to cover their expenses (bills) and then set aside a pre-determined amount of money to invest. Once their bills are taken care of and their investments have been made, then they can spend the remaining money on discretionary items like extra clothing, vacations, etc.

Prioritizing investments over discretionary spending is how the wealthy get ahead. It is not the amount of money one makes that determines whether or not they are wealthy - it is the amount they keep for themselves (through savings and investments) that matters.

There are many middle-class individuals who have become millionaires simply by controlling their expenses and spending habits, while exercising discipline with their investments.

As discussed in the book *The Millionaire Next Door* by Thomas Stanley and William Danko, most millionaires have accumulated their wealth as a result of living below their means and wisely saving and investing their money, rather than spending it all on shiny objects and useless doodads.

Spending all your money on shiny objects and useless doodads like the latest smartphone, clothing you don't need, and adult toys of all types (boats, etc.) doesn't increase your wealth. Instead, it keeps you from becoming wealthy.

It is imperative that you live below your means and pay yourself first by wisely investing and protecting your earnings so that you can accumulate wealth and prosper financially.

Perpetual Wealth

Chapter Ten
Investing In Yourself

One of the best investments you can possibly make in ensuring a prosperous financial future is to invest in yourself. Your future is your responsibility and you are the best asset you have to achieve success in finance and other areas.

Investing in yourself means that you dedicate some of your time and money to educating yourself and giving yourself the means to increase and build your:

- Knowledge
- Financial education
- Confidence
- High income skills

Some examples of how to go about investing in yourself to achieve these goals include:

- Reading financial education books
- Attending professional seminars
- Watching YouTube videos on investing
- Listening to podcasts from successful people
- Learning a new skill

Most people leave education behind once they graduate high school or college and fail to dedicate themselves to lifelong learning. That can hurt them in their later years.

For example, a job layoff in their later career years can leave them scrambling to find a new source of income. Their outdated skills can make it difficult to find a new job and that can hurt their financial security tremendously – if not destroy it altogether.

By continuously investing in your knowledge and skills, you not only make yourself more marketable when it comes to finding a new job, but you also increase your ability to get a raise at your current job. Additionally, the new knowledge and confidence you acquire can make you a smarter investor and may even inspire you to launch your own entrepreneurial venture.

No matter how much wealth you acquire in life, it could all disappear in a short period of time due to theft, loss, lawsuits, and economic downturns. Even if you lose everything you have, you still have your skills and knowledge. If you have that, you stand a much better chance at recovering than others who do not improve their knowledge and skills.

Chapter Eleven
Learn From The Best

Chances are, you weren't taught much about money, finance or investing by your parents. And you likely weren't taught about those topics in school either. That's not exactly a recipe for success in life.

Most people are taught instead to study hard, get a good job, and save for retirement. The steps by which one navigates a world governed by the rules of money, finance, taxes, and investing, however, are not taught. That is a real failure of society today.

If you want to succeed financially, you must take the time and make the effort to learn about money, finance, and investing on your own. Reading this book is a great start, as you're already ahead of the vast majority of the population. Congrats!

When it comes to learning about money, you need to be cognizant about where you get your information and you need to guard yourself against bad information.

I consider it to be wise to learn about topics from multiple people with different viewpoints. This allows me to weigh different options on certain topics and make an informed decision on my own that's right for me, but based on information from others that I deem valuable.

It's also important to be aware of who you spend time with and what their viewpoints on money, financing, and investing are. There's a saying that says the people you spend time with now will determine where you are in a few years.

When we spend time with and learn from our peers, we tend to align ourselves with their views. If you friends aren't on their own mission to become financially free and wealthy, consider what their influence on you will be.

If you want to be successful, you should surround yourself with successful people. If you spend time with people who are careless with their finances, you'll likely find that you're no better off then them.

If you don't have friends that are on the same track as you when it comes to financial planning, have no fear! There are plenty of experts and successful people who have information to share with you.

I read books, listen to podcasts, and watch videos that are authored and created by people far more successful than I am, so that I might learn from their experiences and improve my knowledge.

If you don't have direct access to financially successful people, learn from them from a distance through their teachings.

Great sources of information that can increase your financial education with relation to money, finance, investing, and wealth include:

- Books
- Podcasts
- Seminars
- Online articles
- Online videos on YouTube

A few of the people that I've learned much of my financial knowledge and gained inspiration from include:

- Robert Kiyosaki
- Mike Maloney
- Ray Dalio
- Warren Buffet
- Jim Rickards
- Jim Rogers
- Richard Branson

These people are just a small sample of those who I read about, listen to, and learn from. There are dozens of excellent YouTube channels run by individuals who have succeeded by investing in stocks and real estate, becoming entrepreneurs, or doing side gigs to increase their income. I value their stories and advice as much as I do other more famous people, as everyone has a different take on ways to succeed financially.

If you aren't doing so already, I would urge you to seek out multiple sources of information and viewpoints on building wealth. My opinions are mine, and they may not be right for you. Always do your research and make your own informed decision!

Perpetual Wealth

Section 3 - Wealth Machine Basics

Perpetual Wealth

Chapter Twelve

Why Saving Money Won't Make You Rich

Most of us have all had the same mantra of life drilled into our heads from a young age: Go to school, get a good job, and save for retirement. That's about the extent of what most people know and it's why they'll be in financial trouble down the road.

The problem with saving money is that you lose. Robert Kiyosaki famously writes that "savers are losers". He doesn't mean that people are incompetent in some way. What he means is that people who save their money lose out in the end.

You're probably thinking that those statements are way off base. After all, you've been told to save your whole life. How can it be that savers are losers?

There are three main reasons that saving money makes you lose out on building real wealth:

- **Inflation reduces the purchasing power of savings.** When the cost of living goes up each year, each dollar that you have saved in the bank buys less and less. Your purchasing power diminishes over time.

- **The government prints money, which makes money worth less (or worthless).** Since the government can print and create fiat (e.g. "fake") money at-will, it means the purchasing power of our dollars is worth less and less over time. In fact, if the government prints too much money, our money can become altogether worthless. The government is endangering the purchasing power of your savings when it prints money.

- **Your money isn't working for you when you save.** You've worked for the money that you've been able to save, but your savings aren't working for you. Your money doesn't multiply when it's sitting in the bank getting near-zero interest. Thus, you're always having to work for more money. If, however, you put your money to work in an investment that returns cash flow, your money is working for you.

Grant Cardone – a prominent real estate investor and prominent figure on YouTube – says "cash is trash". I love that line and I agree with him wholeheartedly. Grant, like Robert Kiyosaki, knows that money isn't worth the paper it's printed on. That's why he, Robert, and other wealthy individuals make it their job to buy assets with their money. Assets are far better than money. And assets that produce cash flow (money) are the best assets of all.

Chapter Thirteen
Trading Your Time And Life For Money

Most people spend their entire adult lives slaving away at a job they don't like just to pay their bills. They spend all the money they earn and fail to build savings and investments that can increase their wealth and ensure a secure retirement. Thus, they are wage slaves trapped until they die in a sadistic rat race that they never manage to escape.

A recent Gallup poll found that as much as 85 percent of people hate their jobs. That's an incredibly depressing number when you realize that a person's employment eats up their majority of their waking hours in adult life. Spending the majority of your life doing something you hate doesn't sound like a very fulfilling way to live your life.

If you're a young man or woman just starting out in your career, you might feel enthusiastic about your job and what the future holds for you. However, if you're like the vast majority of your older coworkers, you'll find that you eventually end up hating your job or switching fields altogether one or more times in your life. That means there's a good chance you'll end up working in a field that has nothing to do with your college degree or training. To top that off, chances are that you'll be receiving small pay increases over time unless you increase your skillset immensely and change jobs. How's that for an optimistic look into the future?

From a young age we're all taught to go to school, get good grades, and get a good job. That sounds good in theory. And while education is extremely valuable in life, it's what we're not taught that can really hold us back from achieving a lifetime of happiness and financial security.

Most people do the best they can in school and get the best job they can for the best pay. They focus on getting pay increases to increase their "wealth" as they progress through their career. This strategy doesn't seem to work all that well for most people, as the vast majority of the population fails to build their wealth and ensure their financial prosperity.

So what's the problem with what we've been told? There's a key element to understanding money that we're not taught by society. There's something that the wealthy understand that others don't...

Wealthy people understand that working for money isn't going to make you rich. Instead, they know that working for money keeps you poor.

At this point you're probably thinking I'm completely off base. Those statements make no sense to most people. I'll dive into that in the next chapter.

For the time being, just understand that there's nothing wrong with having a job and earning a paycheck. It's how the vast majority of people get started obtaining their wealth. It's just not the most efficient way to go about things.

The downside to earning your money through a job is that it's time-intensive and can take away from your life in terms of time that you can't otherwise spend with your friends and family, and doing things you find more fulfilling.

While you're earning your money through your job, I think it's imperative that you take time to learn high-income skills. This can make you more valuable in the workplace and increase your pay much more substantially than would otherwise happen if you didn't learn new skills. Constant learning is a key component of life that wealthy people pursue.

Once you obtain more skills, you're able to transition to higher paying jobs. Assuming you control your spending and divert much of your new earnings to savings and investments, that increased pay can substantially improve your financial security and get you on the path to building significant wealth in your lifetime.

When you earn money through a job you're trading your time for money. The downside to that – even if you enjoy your job – is that there are only a certain amount of hours that you can work each week. Thus, there's a cap on how much you can earn. Even though you might earn a lot per hour, you can't obtain unlimited earnings potential through a job.

There are more efficient ways to earn more money than your regular job. Time efficiency is critical to building wealth, as time is limited and the more your harness its potential, the more you can succeed.

You can employ several different methods to start supplementing the earnings from your job and even potentially quit your job if you are able to succeed. I cover some of the methods for generating money efficiently near the end of the book.

Chapter Fourteen
Abundance Through Good Money Habits

I am a firm believer that good money habits are required to attract wealth into your life. Some people call this the law of attraction or refer to it as a spiritual law of money. Whatever your viewpoint on the matter, it is an undeniable truth that good money management is required to build and preserve wealth.

A thousand years ago a person's wealth was determined by the number of sheep they had in their flock. If they looked after, took care of, and protected their sheep, their flock would multiply and their wealth would increase. If they failed to take care of their flock, wolves would kill some of their sheep, disease would kill others, and their wealth would decline.

Similar to the example of sheep, taking care of, looking after, and respecting your money is key to acquiring more money and building your wealth.

If you spend all of the money you bring in each month, you will not have any left to save or invest. When you spend your money today on things you don't really need, you rob yourself of wealth that can provide for you and your family in the future.

The opportunity to generate additional money and increase your investments is only available if you have a pool of money that's been set aside to take advantage of a particular opportunity.

For example, if you are presented with the opportunity to invest in a venture that will produce a return of 10% interest per year, you'll no doubt be interested. But if the minimum investment amount in that venture is $60,000 and you don't have that amount set aside, you'll miss out on the opportunity.

That's an example of how it takes money to make money. And it's why the rich keep getting richer, while the poor and middle class struggle. The rich have built up cash reserves for themselves, while the poor and middle class have little or none.

If you live below your means and practice good money management by setting aside some of your income for future investments, you give yourself the opportunity to make more money and build your wealth.

If you had the opportunity to make additional side income of $40/hour at night, you might be interested in pursuing that gig. But if you have to stay at home at night to watch after your children, you can't take that gig unless you've set some money aside. If you do have money in reserve, you can hire a babysitter at a rate of $15/hour and do the side gig for $40/hour, which results in a net profit of $25/hour of extra income for you. That's an example of using your money to bring in more money.

When you use your money wisely, you are respecting and honoring it, which can lead to greater financial abundance in your life.

If, conversely, you spend money unwisely and fail to keep some in reserve, you are not respecting your money or practicing good money habits. That will keep you from building lasting wealth.

Whether or not you believe so yourself, it's clear to me that there is a spiritual law of money that's in effect and influences your ability to build and preserve your wealth.

Even if you disagree, you have to admit it's easy to see that using your money wisely is a key component of attracting more money, abundance, and wealth into your life.

Perpetual Wealth

Chapter Fifteen
Precursors To Building Wealth

To effectively build lasting wealth, you must first free yourself of financial liabilities. That means paying off bad debt (credit cards, student loans, etc), developing an emergency savings fund, and building an opportunity fund for investments.

It makes no sense to try and invest when your investment returns are lower than higher rate credit card debt you may be carrying. Pay off bad debt as quickly as possible so you can move on to the next phase of financial freedom – building your wealth.

Building an emergency savings fund that can provide a lifeboat of safety when stormy waters appear is crucial. If you have an unexpected expense arise and you don't have any reserve savings set aside for emergencies, you're either going to have to go in debt or tap into your investments. Neither of these options are a good thing,

Many experts advise that you have an emergency savings fund that contains enough money to cover a minimum of three months of living expenses. Others recommend an emergency savings fund of six to twelve months worth of living expenses. The amount of funds you keep for emergencies is up to you. It's important to remember that the emergency funds are just for emergencies. Keep emergency funds separate from other accounts to prevent yourself from spending them on non-emergency items.

This is not a book about how to get out of debt, but the basic steps of doing so are quite simple:

- Reduce your discretionary spending
- Lower your expenses
- Increase your income
- Use the money left over to pay down your debt

The more effectively you can do each of those steps, the faster you'll get out of debt.

It's painful to direct excess income to pay down debt, but the freedom of being debt-free and being able to build your wealth is a truly amazing experience.

Once you're free of bad debt and have emergency and opportunity funds up, you're ready to proceed to a really exciting step – building your wealth!

.

Chapter Sixteen
Types Of Income

Tantamount to the building of wealth is income. Without it, there is no mathematical equation to developing wealth. Most people think of income as what they earn from their job. That's one type of income, but it's the least efficient and the most time-intensive when compared to others. Understanding the different types of income allows you to setup your strategy for investing in assets that produce income.

The main types of different income that can build your wealth are as follows:

- **Earned Income**. This is how most people start building wealth. It's the money you receive for having a job and working for someone else. This is the least efficient and most time-intensive way of making money and has the fewest tax benefits.

- **Business Income**. This is profits from a business that you run and own. Business income can often produce the highest levels of income if you have the right product or service. There are several tax benefits with a business that can reduce your tax bill through deductions.

- **Residual Income**. This is profit that you continue to receive from a business that you do not (or no longer) actively operate. If you hire someone to run your business or are a non-participating partial owner of a business, you have residual income.

- **Interest Income**. This is income that you receive from certificates of deposit (CDs), treasury bills, or personal lending.

- **Dividend Income**. This is income that you receive from stock dividends.

- **Rental Income**. This is income that you receive from residential or commercial rental properties, storage units, or other types of property.

- **Royalty Income**. This is income you receive from licensing a brand, product, or idea to another company for production or distribution.

- **Capital Gains Income**. This is income you receive from selling stocks, properties, collectibles, and fixed assets. Different tax rates are applied to short-term capital gains and long-term capital gains. Capital gains doesn't provide ongoing income like the other methods unless you sell assets on a regular basis.

Understanding these different types of income and how to leverage them is critical to mapping out and deploying your strategy for building wealth.

Having multiple streams of income of different types is ideal for ensuring the fastest route to building wealth. Trading your time for income (e.g. through a job) is the most time-intensive method of generating wealth. Thus, I would recommend focusing your attention on building additional streams of income from different methods.

There's nothing wrong with generating income from a job, but it is the least efficient in terms of time and effort. When you start out building wealth using income from a job, focus your efforts on ways to increase your salary, lowering your expenses, and increasing your investments in different assets that produce income streams that are not tied to your time and effort.

Towards the end of this book I provide some guidance and examples of ways to generate additional income more efficiently than trading your time for money. If you want to increase your income in the most efficient way possible, make sure to read that chapter.

Perpetual Wealth

Chapter Seventeen
Why The Rich Don't Work For Money

The wealthy understand that working for money isn't very effective in building their wealth. They understand that when you trade your time for money, you're trading your life for something that isn't worth all that much.

With inflation and the government increasing the money supply by printing money, money isn't worth all that much. While they may have a lot of money, money isn't the thing the wealthy work for in and of itself.

What do the wealthy work for? Put simply, the wealthy work for assets instead of money.

They work for assets that have real value and that produce income for them. They work for assets that build their wealth without being directly correlated to the amount of time they put into building their wealth.

The rich don't work for money. They work for assets that produce money.

The rich understand that when they work for and obtain assets, their assets are working to produce money. They know that assets can produce money without a direct relation to the time they put into them. They understand the efficiency in this. And they understand the financial security, wealth, freedom, and opportunities this provides them.

The poor do not understand this. The poor work hard for money, focus their efforts of making more money, and use their money to buy shiny doodads that are not assets. The poor stay poor because they don't understand the value of real assets.

The rich work for assets, while the poor work for money. That's a critical distinction that makes all the difference in the world when it comes to building true wealth.

Chapter Eighteen
Invest In Assets Not Liabilities

Understanding what real assets are is extremely important in building one's wealth. Most people think they're buying assets, when they're really buying liabilities. They're spending their hard-earned money on things that won't bring them true wealth.

Many people think they have assets, when in fact they really have liabilities. Let's take a look at what real assets and liabilities are.

Here's the simple version:

- **An <u>asset</u> puts money <u>in</u> your pocket**
- **A <u>liability</u> takes money <u>out of</u> your pocket**

It's really that simple. There are some exceptions to the definition of an asset that I'll cover, but the definitions above are the general rule the wealthy use when determining whether something is an asset or a liability.

Your House Is Not An Asset

When people say their house is an asset, they're misinformed. If they lost their job and their income stopped coming in, they'd realize just how much of a liability their house is. They'd still have to pay the mortgage, insurance, utilities, and upkeep. Their house would take money out of their pocket – it would not put money in their pocket.

There's nothing wrong with buying a home. It's a great place to raise your family and live your life, but your house is not really an asset.

Many people believe their house is an asset if it appreciates in value and they sell it for more than they bought it for. While this can be true, it assumes that the house appreciates and that someone is willing to buy it for more than it was originally purchased for. As was the case in the financial crisis, home prices can plummet when the economy goes south.

Additionally, selling your house for a profit only adds to your wealth if you are downsizing into a less expensive house. If you don't do that, you don't really realize any increase in your wealth due to the sale of your house.

In general, your primary residence can be viewed as a type of asset that helps you <u>preserve</u> your wealth and improve your quality of life. In that sense, it is an asset. In other ways, it is not an asset.

Your Car And Possessions Are Not Assets

Your vehicle and other possessions depreciate (decrease in value) the moment you start using them. There are a few exceptions to this, but most people assume the stuff they have are assets, when in fact they are not.

Assets That Cash Flow

The best assets are the ones that put money in your pocket. This is called positive cash flow. The more assets you own that produce income streams for you, the larger the cash flow you have coming in.

When you use your money to buy assets that produce cash flow, you are increasing your wealth. When you do this, you are not only buying an asset, you are increasing your income stream as well. This is one of the best ways to build and preserve wealth.

Some examples of real assets that provide cash flow include:

- Rental properties that produce rental income
- Businesses that return profits
- Stocks that pay dividends

Assets That Increase In Value

Some assets appreciate (increase in value) over time (or at least that's the hope). This is called capital appreciation and it's what most people aim for when they invest in the stock market.

However, there's no guarantee that your assets will increase in value over time. A stock market correction or crash can severely affect the value of your stock portfolio and leave you in a financially unstable position – especially if it happens as you near retirement.

That's why the wealthy often prefer assets that cash flow over assets that might (or might not) experience a capital gain.

Some examples of assets that can increase in value over time (but might not) include:

- Stocks
- Real estate
- Farmland
- Collector cars
- Collector baseball cards and comic books
- Old stamps, currency, and rare coins

Assets That Preserve Wealth

Another type of asset is one that preserves your wealth, or at least helps protect your wealth from serious deterioration.

Some examples of assets that can help to preserve your wealth over time include:

- Real estate
- Farmland

- Precious metals

To some extent, most assets that have the potential to increase in value over time also have the ability to help preserve your wealth. However, since the prices of assets can vary over time, there's no guarantee as to what extent any particular asset can protect your wealth.

Land and real estate have been some of the best ways to preserve wealth, as they provide real utilitarian value to others. When it comes to land, there's a limited supply and there will always be real value in owning it.

Precious metals like gold and silver have been used since ancient times as a way of preserving wealth. These metals are still used today by the wealthy and by governments to ensure their continuing wealth.

The Law Of Thirds

Wealth preservation using assets is nothing new. It's been used in different formats for thousands of years.

In medieval times, wealthy families would protect and build their wealth by dividing up their investments roughly as follows:

- One third **land**
- One third **gold**
- One third **art**

That strategy would allow them to preserve their wealth in times of turmoil. If a neighboring country was attacking theirs, they could take their art out of the frames, roll it up, and put it in their saddlebags along with their gold and the deed to their land.

When they arrived safely somewhere else, they could take out their gold and their art and they still had the bulk of their wealth with them. With the deed to their land, they could reclaim it after a period of peace was restored. Sometimes that might have taken a generation or more, but the deed and title to their land offered them and their family a chance to get back what was once theirs.

The importance of preserving your wealth cannot be understated. Once you start to build your wealth, you need to ensure that you protect it with reasonable means while at the same time allowing it to grow.   Methods for accomplishing this will be discussed in later chapters.

Chapter Nineteen
Why Cash Flow Is King

Cash flow is the golden key to building and preserving lasting wealth. It is the engine of your wealth machine. Each asset that you have that generates positive cash flow is a wealth machine in and of itself. When you combine those individual cash flow machines together, you have a solid mega-machine of wealth that can become unstoppable given enough time and care.

A wise bit of advice that the wealthy follow is to not spend the principal of their investments. Instead, they spend only the income (or a portion thereof) that is generated from their cash-flowing investments.

Any portion of that income that isn't used for spending is then put back into the same or other investment to increase their cash flow further. This process allows their cash flow, spending power, and investing power to increase over time.

The strategy of spending only the income from an investment, and not the principal of the investment, is the key to long-lasting wealth.

Traditional investment advice doesn't follow this strategy. Instead, people are often told that they should build up their stock portfolio and assets before retirement and then start drawing them down while in retirement. This behavior decreases an individuals net worth over time and presents a retiree with the risk of running out of money in old age.

A far superior method of ensuring financial security in retirement and in pre-retirement years is to build up one's cash flowing assets such that the total income coming from those investments exceed their living expenses and lifestyle.

If one can accomplish that before they retire, they are almost all but assured that they will not run out of money in retirement, and that they can pass their wealth on to their heirs.

I invest in different types of assets for wealth preservation, appreciation and cash flow, but cash flow is my primary objective when investing.   Why?

Having positive cash flow from my investments means that I am essentially generating my own money. Or more correctly, my investments – which I purchased with money - are making me money. And they make money whether I'm sleeping or awake.

This strategy of buying assets that provide positive cash flow is sometimes referred to as "private banking" or "family banking" because money is seemingly being created from thin air – just like with the real banks. When you have this power in your grasp, you are essentially your own bank. That's an incredibly freeing and powerful experience. That's why cash flow is king.

Chapter Twenty
Never Spend The Principal

I mentioned this already in the previous chapter, but the topic of preserving the principal of your investments is so vital that it deserves its own chapter.

The vital key in building perpetual wealth is recurring cash flow. This cash flow can come from dividend payments, rental income, or any other cash flowing asset. It is only through the investment assets that you acquire over time that this automatic cash flow originates.

In order to ensure cash flow now and in the future, you must protect the asset that produces the cash flow. Thus, selling part of the asset or spending some or all of the principal in the investment endangers your future wealth.

As you spend the principal or sell the asset, your cash flow generating capabilities decrease. This is a recipe for diminishing your wealth and should be avoided at all costs.

The wisest way to ensure perpetual wealth is to ensure that you spend less money that what you have coming in. Thus, you should not spend the entire cash flow that comes from your investments.

Theoretically, you <u>could</u> spend all the cash that comes your way from your assets. However, doing so will leave you unable to increase your cash flow investments and may lead to trouble if the cash flow slows down for a period of time.

If you are serious about creating perpetual wealth for yourself and your family, never degrade your wealth by spending the principal. Only spend the interest and earnings you receive. Only spend the cash flow.

Chapter Twenty-One
Allocating Income To Build Wealth

Building your wealth requires a significant investment of time, effort, and money. In order to achieve lasting wealth, you must take a disciplined approach to how you save and how you invest.

Most people spend all their monthly income and have little or nothing left at the end of the month to save or invest. This is a recipe for disaster when it comes to a financial security, a comfortable retirement, and lasting wealth.

Building wealth is based on the irrefutable laws of mathematics and you cannot cheat the system, no matter how much you desire to skip the prerequisite steps.

Committing to building wealth is just that – a commitment. You must apply yourself to saving and investing on a regular basis to accomplish substantial wealth.

How much or little you dedicate to building wealth is ultimately up to you. However, it helps to have some guidance in the process.

Dan Lok, a successful entrepreneur and YouTube sensation, proposes what I consider a solid plan for allocating your income to succeed financially.

Dan suggests that the following allocation of income for those earning under $100k per year is a good starting point for income allocation:

- **60% for living expenses.** These are the expenses required for life – including your rent or mortgage, utility bills, car payments, food, etc.

- **10% for "fun money".** This is the money you have to splurge on new clothes, vacations, or eating out. We all need to treat ourselves occasionally, but most people spend all of their disposable income in this category. You must exercise restraint in spending your money on shiny doodads if you want to succeed in building wealth.

- **10% for investing in yourself.** This is money you spend on improving your knowledge and skillset. You can do that by buying books, attending seminars, and other activities that improve you in multiple ways. Investing in yourself is one of the best investments you can make in your lifetime.

- **10% for investing in assets.** This is money that you set aside for investing in real estate, the stock market, and other assets.

- **10% for savings.** This is your emergency savings and your opportunity funds. Developing your savings allows you to weather the financial storms that you will encounter at one point in time. It also allows you to acquire assets and take advantage of new investing opportunities when you find them.

If your income exceeds $100k per year, you should be allocating a substantially higher percentage to investments. Wealthy people allocate the vast majority of their income to investments that continue to build their wealth at faster and faster rates.

If you're thinking there's no way you can survive on allocating 60% of your income to living expenses, you should to take a hard look at your financial situation. You either need to downsize your expenses or you need to increase your income if you want to build your wealth. However you accomplish it, you must have enough free cash allocated to savings and investments or you won't get ahead financially.

Perpetual Wealth

Chapter Twenty-Two
Making Your Money Work For You

Most people work for money. They go to school, get the highest paying job they can find, and hope to increase their earned income as their career progresses.

The wealthy do not work for money. Instead, the wealthy work to acquire assets that can generate money for them. In this way, the wealthy do not have to trade their time for money as the poor do.

Once a person acquires enough cash flowing assets that generate income that exceeds their expenses, they have achieved wealth. They are financially free, unlike the masses of people that are trapped in jobs they find unfulfilling.

Acquiring cash flowing assets is the key to building lasting wealth. It is the real life version of the Monopoly board game you probably played as a child. The key to winning that game was to acquire enough assets that would generate enough cash flow to exceed your expenses. If you can accomplish that in real life, you've won the game of financial freedom. Robert Kiyosaki refers to this as escaping the "rat race".

When it comes to investing, most people focus on buying stocks or real estate that they hope will appreciate in value over time. While there's nothing inherently wrong with that approach, it's a speculative proposition unless those assets also provide regular cash flow.

There's no guarantee that an asset will increase in value over time, and that makes hoping for appreciation a gamble. Past stock market and real estate market crashes have proven that things don't always appreciate.

The wealthy view appreciation (capital gains) as a bonus when they invest, but they don't count on it as being a given.

If your stock and real estate investments produce positive cash flow for you, that is a winning strategy for ensuring a path to achieving true wealth. That is the key to winning game of financial freedom and security.

Chapter Twenty-Three
Time Is Of The Essence

When it comes to building wealth, the only real limiting factor is time. You can always find additional ways to increase your income, or new assets to invest it, but you can't create more time. We're all allotted a certain amount of time on this earth and we can't get more than 24 hours in a day.

The importance of time when it comes to building wealth cannot be overstated. The earlier you start at building your wealth, the more time you'll have for that wealth to multiply. If you don't start until you're on the edge of retirement, you likely won't have time to build your wealth substantially.

When you have time on your side you can leverage the power of compounding returns. That means taking the earnings (the interest or dividends) from the investment and re-investing those earnings back into the investment.

For example, if you invest $1,000 in an asset that provides an ongoing return of 4% and you re-invest those earnings back into the asset, the total value of your investment is nearly $4,500 after 30 years. That's without adding any more principal contributions to the asset – just the earnings.

The graphic below, generated using the compound growth calculator at https://mdm.ca shows the growth of the $1,000 investment to nearly $4,500 over a period of 30 years.

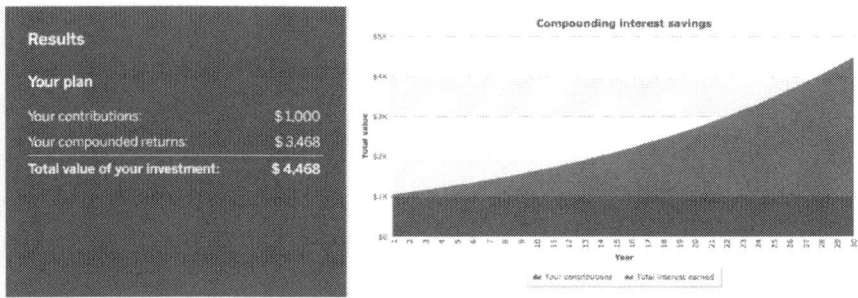

If you only have 10 years to allow that investment to grow, the results are very different. Instead of growing to nearly $4,500 over 30 years, the investment will only grow to approximately $1,650 over 10 years.

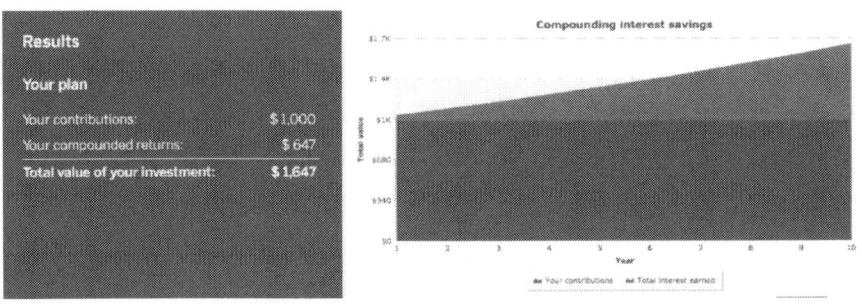

This is why time is so important when it comes to building your wealth. Leveraging the power of compound returns over time can greatly increase your wealth. Albert Einstein referred to compounding returns as the "eighth wonder of the world" and I certainly agree with him on that.

Perpetual Wealth

If you continue to contribute on a regular (i.e. monthly) basis, your investment will continue to grow with the combination of your earnings and your regularly invested principle.

The graphic below shows how contributing $1,000 per month into an asset that produces an annual return of 4% can result in a total value of almost $700,000 after 30 years. That's close to double the amount of total principal ($360,000) you invested into the asset.

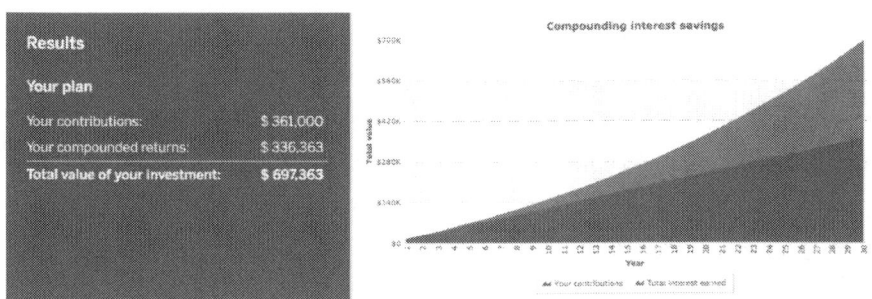

Once you reach a point where you are no longer contributing new principal to an asset, you can begin to use the earnings from that asset to cover your expenses.

Using the example above and starting with a total investment value of $697,000 that earns 4% returns in future years, you would end up with annual earnings of approximately $27,800. That equates to earnings of over $2,300 per month.

If, after taxes, you're able to cover all your expenses, you will have reached a point where you are now financially free and able to live off the earnings of your investment, rather than having to use the principal of the earnings to support yourself.

Assuming a constant rate of return of 4%, the investment would continue to provide you with pre-tax earnings of over $2,300 per month in perpetuity.

That's a simple example of a "money machine" that provides cash flow and builds your wealth. Combined with other money machines that provide cash flowing returns, you can achieve a lifetime of financial freedom that ensures you never run out of money.

This is why the rich invest in assets that provide cash flow. With enough money machines, they can grow their wealth and live life on their terms without having to work for money like the poor and middle-class do. Their money works for them.

Chapter Twenty-Four
Class Is In Session

An important step in building your wealth is understanding asset classes. Broadly speaking, asset classes are different distinct types of investment assets. Each class of assets has its own unique characteristics that have different risk/reward tradeoffs and different desirability factors for investors.

Most people aren't really aware of different asset classes outside of the stock market. The reason for this is lack of formal education on finance and wealth. They haven't been taught about the different asset classes that are available, their benefits, or their risks.

For reference, here are some of the most popular and well-known asset classes that exist:

- Cash
- Stocks
- Real estate
- Farmland
- Business
- Lending
- Cryptocurrency
- Precious metals
- Collectibles

This is by no means an exhaustive list of asset classes that are available – it's just a starting point. Some of the many other asset classes that exist include timberland, oil and gas exploration, and fine art. The topics in this book will concentrate on the main asset classes listed above.

Understanding the different asset classes that are available helps immensely when it comes to diversifying your investments and preserving your wealth. You can allocate your investments based on different risk factors and end goals using different asset classes.

Each class of assets has different characteristics that can help you achieve your goals. I'll cover the main highlights of each asset class, and give you concrete examples of how you can invest in each asset class later in the book.

Chapter Twenty-Five
Liquid Gold

Liquidity is an important concept in investing. It is essentially your ability to convert an investment to cash or cash equivalent easily.

Investments that can quickly and easily be sold and converted to cash are referred to as highly liquid, whereas those that cannot be sold and converted to cash are called illiquid. Many assets lie somewhere between being highly liquid and illiquid.

Having a level of liquidity in your investments is critical. It allows you to sell part of all of your investments for cash to cover expenses or buy a different type of investment easily.

The exact level of liquidity for various types of assets and investments will differ, but a general summary of liquidity for some common asset classes is given below for reference.

Asset Type	Liquidity	Notes
Bank Accounts	Very Liquid	Cash in your bank accounts is the definition of liquid.
Stocks	High Liquidity	Easily sold and converted to cash.
Real Estate (Physical)	Low Liquidity	Physical real estate investments take time to sell. Some investments have lock-in periods.

Asset Type	Liquidity	Notes
Real Estate (REITs)	Somewhat Liquid	Withdrawal of funds can be simple, difficult, or impossible, depending on the investment.
Farmland	Low Liquidity	Similar attributes to physical real estate.
Lending	Somewhat Liquid	Cashing out will depend on length of the loan. Portions of loan might be able to be withdrawn occasionally.
Cryptocurrency	High Liquidity	Easily sold and converted to cash.
Precious Metals (Physical)	Somewhat Liquid	Physical coins have to be sold in person or online, which can cause delays.
Precious Metals (Virtual)	High Liquidity	ETFs and vaulted metals can be sold and converted to cash quickly.
Collectibles	Somewhat Liquid	Sale may have to be done in person. Limited market may slow sale.

The liquidity guidelines listed in the table above will vary depending on the specific details of a particular investment, so don't treat those as hard rules. Make sure you understand the level of liquidity you can expect before you make any specific investment.

Many people are afraid of investing in things that aren't considered highly liquid. If you're used to keeping your money parked in a bank account or invested in the stock market, locking your money up in an investment that has low or no liquidity can seem frightening.

I view lower liquidity investments differently. As long as I have a significant percentage of my investments in liquid or highly liquid assets, I feel comfortable investing in things with low liquidity.

Why? There are two main reasons. First, sometimes the investments with the best returns have low liquidity. Second, I like having some of my investments fairly inaccessible to me. The fact that I can't sell or exit them quickly ensures that I'm not tempted to spend the value of the investment unwisely.

Investing is a long-term game and forcing yourself to leave some of your assets in that game for a longer period of time can be beneficial. However, maintaining a high level of liquidity for a portion of your investments is important in the event you need money to cover expenses or if you have the opportunity to acquire new assets at a discount.

Your level of comfort with liquidity will affect your investing strategy. You can develop an effective investment portfolio utilizing only highly liquid assets, but it offers fewer options than one that contains assets of varying levels of liquidity.

Keeping a portion of your money in the bank allows you a great deal of financial flexibility. Not only will cash in the bank provide you with a sense of security, but it will allow you to act quickly an purchase assets when you find new investment opportunities. If all of your investments are locked up and illiquid, you won't have much ability to jump on the opportunity to acquire new investment assets.

When keeping money in the banking system, I highly recommend using multiple accounts to separate your funds by their intended purpose. For example, I use different accounts for:

- Usual expenses and everyday purchases
- Emergency savings
- Opportunity funds

Your opportunity fund is spare cash that you have available to acquire new assets that you feel are good investments. If you do not maintain some level of opportunity fund, your ability to acquire new assets and invest in new opportunities is limited.

The exact amount you leave in the bank as an opportunity fund will vary. Some guidelines recommend having one third of your assets in liquid or highly liquid form. You might consider keeping 10-20% of your net worth in cash for new opportunities, but the exact percentage is up to you.

Once you use part of your opportunity fund to acquire new assets, work on replenishing it so you're prepared for the next investment opportunity that comes your way.

Liquidity – whether it's through a dedicated opportunity fund or other type of asset – is an important thing to have. You never know when you're going to need cash, or for what purpose, so it's always good to have flexibility. As they say, preparation is the key to success.

Chapter Twenty-Six
Accredited Advantage

It's no secret that government regulations can often have a negative impact on everyday people. Regulations that are often touted as protecting people often place limitations on their access to activities, goods, and services that would otherwise improve their lives. Government involvement with regards to investing is no different.

After the stock market crash of 1929, people were furious that they lost a good portion or all of their investments in the stock market. They clamored for the government to protect them, and the government took action – although it ended up hurting more than helping.

In 1933 Congress passed the Securities Act, which limited some "risky" investments to what it called "accredited investors" who had a high net worth. The reasoning for this was that high net worth investors had enough financial resources to fend for themselves and invest in assets that were deemed risky.

What I imagine probably happened behind close doors was that the politicians thought the public was crazy. People wanted high returns, but without the risk. People wanted to be protected, but they wanted to profit at the same time. The government knew this wasn't possible. They knew the public was crazy. But the people wanted action, so the government needed to act.

And so, with the passing of the Securities Act, government touted that they were protecting people, when they knew they were not. In truth, the Securities Act pushed the middle class out of having the ability to invest in certain assets that could make them wealthy.

After the financial crisis of 2008, the people demanded more protection from Wall Street and the banks. Again, the government answered their request with new regulations. And again, the regulation hurt the middle class.

In response to the 2008 financial crisis, Congress passed the "Dodd-Frank Wall Street Reform and Consumer Protection Act" in 2010. One of the provisions in that law hurt the middle class again.

Prior to 2010, people were allowed to include the value of their primary residence as part of their net worth for investing purposes. After 2010, they were not able to do so. This further hurt the ability of the middle class to invest in assets that could build their wealth.

Having a high net worth makes you eligible to become what's known as an accredited investor. Accredited investors have access to more investment options that non-accredited investors do, and the investments they have access to often offer better returns and, in many cases, better protection that other investments.

As of 2019, the definition of an accredited investor is as follows:

- An individual who makes $200,00 or more per year
- A couple filing jointly that makes $300,00 or more per year
- Someone who has a net worth of $1,000,000 or more (excluding the value of their house)

Being able to meet the accredited investor guidelines is important to building wealth, as it opens up more options to you for investing. Some of the investments I cover later in this book are available only to accredited investors.

If you don't meet the accredited investor guidelines now, I'd suggest focusing on building your assets and increasing your income one step at a time. As your income and assets increase over time, you stand a good chance at meeting the accredited investor guidelines.

Even if you can't meet the accredited investor guidelines, you can still build lasting wealth and financial security, so don't fret about not being an accredited investors.

Perpetual Wealth

Chapter Twenty-Seven
The Wealth Machine Blueprint

Building lasting wealth means ensuring you never run out money – no matter how long you live. It also means that you can leave your wealth to future generations. If they use it wisely, they will never run out of money either.

This is an incredible gift to give your children, so long as you teach them the value of money, how to use money wisely, how to keep the wealth machine working, and how to teach their heirs how to do the same. If this can be accomplished, it is called multi-generational wealth.

Here's the basic blueprint for building your own wealth machine:

- **Allocate a portion of your income to investing in assets**. If you don't do this, you can't invest in assets.

- **Invest in assets that produce positive cash flow**. These are money machines. Your money is now working for you to make more money while you sleep.

- **Reinvest earnings into the same or different assets that produce positive cash flow**. This increases the capital in the investment and increases cash flow from the asset.

- **Allow the power of time and compounding returns increase your wealth.** Patience is required, but the laws of mathematics work in your favor if you have time.

- **Spend only a portion of the cash flow that comes from your investments.** When it comes time to relying on your investments to cover your expenses and support your lifestyle, make sure you preserve the principal invested so as to ensure that the asset will continue to provide ongoing cash flow.

That's it. It's really that simple. Most people don't understand these basic steps and don't take the time to learn. You're already way ahead of the game compared to them.

Future chapters will cover different assets that you can invest in that produce positive cash flow, as well as assets that preserve and protect your wealth.

Chapter Twenty-Eight
Send Out Your Army

Go To War

The money you have is your army. To win the battle of financial freedom and perpetual wealth, you must send your money to war. If soldiers sit idle, they lose their skills. If your money sits idle, it loses its purchasing power.

Expect Casualties

In war, casualties are a given. No matter what kind of investments you make over time, you will surely have losses. This is a given. You must accept this fact.

Take Prisoners

In war, your goal is to have your money win battles and bring back prisoners. Every dollar your investments earn is a prisoner that comes back to you. Enlist that prisoner in your army and send it back out to fight another battle and take more prisoners.

Some Battles Will Be Lost

You're going to lose some battles in war. You're going to lose some of your money in some of your investments. But your end goal is not to win every battle – it is to win the war of financial freedom and perpetual wealth.

Fight From Multiple Fronts

Wars are not fought on a single front. Wars are fought on multiple fronts using similar tactics and a variety of methods. Put your army of money to the task of fighting your wealth war on multiple fronts, leveraging the asset classes and diversification strategies that fit your war plan.

Let Others Fight For You

You might have to be directly involved in your wealth war at the start by earning money at a job. As your army of money grows, you can have your money do the hard work of winning battles, taking prisoners, and increasing your wealth for you.

Monitor The Battles

Generals monitor the progress and outcome of battles, adjust their strategy, and plan future attacks. It is important you monitor your investments, adjust your strategies, and deploy your army of money appropriately so it can achieve your goals.

Reserves

Not every single soldier is sent out to battle. Some are kept in reserve in case all is lost, so other attacks can be launched. In investing, make sure to keep some of your money in reserve (savings) for emergency and opportunity funds.

Allies

Fighting wars requires allies and advisors. Seek wise counsel in your investments, learn about money and finance on a regular basis, find new investments, and leverage your resources in your financial war.

Celebrate The Victory

Once you've won the war of financial freedom and perpetual wealth, you can enjoy the victory of your work and the work of your money. Cherish the victory, but do not forget the work that was involved in winning the war. Always remember the costs associated with the war, honor those who have helped you, and help others who are fighting their own wars.

Perpetual Wealth

Section 4

-

Wealth Diversification

Perpetual Wealth

Chapter Twenty-Nine
The Importance Of Diversification

When I was a kid, my parents taught me to never put all my eggs in one basket. That early introduction to diversification has stuck with me through life and has greatly influenced the manner in which I invest today.

Many people fail to understand diversification or appreciate its value. The core principle of diversification is to help ensure that your investments stand a good chance of surviving economic downturns or crashes specific to a particular asset class or individual asset.

A solid understanding of diversification is required to acquire lasting wealth. By building your wealth machines in such a way as to leverage diversification, you can be assured that your wealth is protected far better than without it.

For most people, the introduction of the concept of – and usually the only knowledge of – diversification is limited to stocks, bonds, and mutual funds. The phrase "well-diversified portfolio" means very little to most people, as their understanding of how to structure their retirement portfolio is limited to the stock market and they have little to no awareness of other asset classes they could invest in.

Alas, even with some knowledge of the stock market, people are rarely taught or made aware of the differences between ETFs, index funds, growth stocks, and dividend stocks.

Altogether, the lack of financial education in our country and elsewhere is astonishing. And it comes with a heavy price.

When it comes to investing for their future, most people place all their trust in other companies and people. They rarely question what they're told and they all too often fail to educate themselves on other options or opinions that are out there. This leaves them exposed to a single asset class, unaware of the potential danger they may face down the road.

Your level of diversification will depend on your knowledge of the options that are available, your tolerance for risk, and your belief in the future outcome of a specific investment strategy. There is no one "right" option for everyone. Each individual has unique goals for their future and each person must make an informed decision on their own accord.

As you continue through this book, you'll see that I employ a hyper-diversified investment strategy. I'll explain why I follow the strategy I do, why I believe certain types of investments are good, and what I believe my overall strategy can provide. While my strategy may not be right for your particular situation, I hope it offers insights to options and methods of investing that you were not previously aware of.

Chapter Thirty
A Strategy For Diversification

When the subject of diversifying investments comes up, most people think only about a portfolio of stocks, bonds, and mutual funds. That's because it's all they've been told about with regards to investing and diversification.

As I've outlined in previous chapters, there are many other options for investing other than the stock market. If you choose to invest in multiple options, your ability to diversify your assets increases.

There is no one specific investment and diversification strategy that works for everyone. Your investment and diversification strategy will be unique to your needs and goals.

I was taught at a young age to never put all my eggs in one basket. I've taken that to heart with my investment strategy. The strategy I use is one that is hyper-diversified across different asset classes, companies, and risk/reward factors.

The manner in which I diversify my assets provides me with the assurance that my wealth:

- Grows over time
- Provides stable cash flow

- Is resilient to economic downturns
- Is protected against loss or deterioration

My strategy for diversifying assets may not be right for you. You have to evaluate your own situation and goals and make your own decisions as to how to invest and diversify.

It is important to understand that my investment and diversification strategy changes over time based on a number of factors including:

- My near term and long term goals
- The current economic environment
- Indicators of future economic outlook
- New investment opportunities I find
- New knowledge that I gain on finances and investing

Having the ability to change direction in your investment strategy is important. Your goals and other factors may require you to change your strategy over time, so make sure to re-evaluate your strategy on a regular basis and make the changes you deem appropriate.

In an effort to protect and grow my wealth, I diversify my investments across several different asset classes, including:

- Cash
- Stocks, bonds, and mutual funds
- Businesses
- Real estate
- Farmland
- Peer to peer lending

- Cryptocurrency
- Precious metals
- Collectibles
- Miscellaneous alternative assets

This diversification strategy allows me to balance risk and reward, protect my wealth, and grow it over time.

The reason I take this approach is my desire to attain a high level of resilience against market downturns, economic cycles, and other factors. A failure or significant downturn in any single asset class has limited impact on my overall wealth since I spread my investments over multiple asset classes. This is the high-level diversification of my investment "eggs" across multiple "baskets".

As I discover new assets and asset classes to invest in, I make additional investments across those to continue my overall strategy of diversification. This allows me to maintain a hyper-diversified investment strategy that I believe is key to maintaining resilience.

Diversifying across several asset classes isn't where I stop. I take it ever further, with multiple levels of diversification. For example, within each asset class I continue to diversify in the following ways:

- By company, provider, or individual
- By location
- By type, format, or other attribute

Some high level examples of how I invest within specific asset classes are as follows...

For my stock market investments, I diversify my investments across:

- Different brokerages and investment platforms
- Different market segments
- Stocks from different companies
- Dividend and growth stocks

For my precious metals investments, I diversify across:

- A mix of ETFs and physical bullion
- Different types and sizes of precious metals
- Different dealers and brokers
- Different geographic locations and storage facilities

I go into more detailed examples of how I diversify within each asset class - as well as why I invest in specific asset classes - in later chapters. Each asset class is unique and requires a different strategy with regards to diversification.

I have some core beliefs that drive my overall hyper-diversification strategy:

- **Never trust in any one thing,** because a specific investment or asset class may not be valuable or viable at a future date.
- **Never trust in any one company,** because even good companies can go bankrupt and bad ones can scam others.
- **Never trust in any one person**, because people can pass on bad information, relationships can change, and trust can be lost.

- **Never trust in any one viewpoint,** because no one knows for certain which viewpoint is correct. I always evaluate different viewpoints and come to my own conclusion.
- **Never trust in any one outcome**, because the future is not certain. What seems like a sure thing today could be gone tomorrow.

When I say I "never trust" any one thing, person, company, etc. I simply mean that I do not place 100% of my trust in that thing, person, or company. I wouldn't be investing in different assets, working with different companies, or following a specific strategy if I didn't have a reasonable level of trust in them.

Trust is important, but trust must be gained over time, and even when we think we can trust someone or something, things can always go wrong. That's why I always weigh my options and hedge my bets.

For example, some people say gold is a safe store of value and others say it's a relic of the past. Some people say owning physical gold is the best, while others say gold ETFs are the best. Some people think cryptocurrency is the future of the financial system and an excellent investment, while others think is a speculative bubble with no long-term value.

There are a multitude of different opinions out there when it comes to investing. In the end, no one knows for certain what the best method of investing is for everyone and no one knows what the future holds. This is why I take time to evaluate different viewpoints, strategies, companies, and assets before I act.

It is only after I consider different options and possible outcomes that I can come to a strategy that is something I'm confident is in line with my goals.

Chapter Thirty-One
Asset Allocation

Think And Act Like The Wealthy

When the subject of diversifying investments comes up, most people think only of diversification as relating to a portfolio of stocks, bonds, and mutual funds. The reason for this is they haven't been taught about other asset classes or other ways to diversify.

While the wealthy may have a significant portion of their wealth in the stock market, that's not the only place they invest. Wealthy people hedge their bets and spread their wealth across several asset classes.

As I've stated before, the wealthy have a wealthy mindset, while the poor and middle class have a poor mindset. Investing all your financial assets in a single asset (e.g. the stock market) is a poor mindset.

If you want to become wealthy, you should pay attention to what they wealthy do and how they think. That's why research and education are so important. By investing in yourself and increasing your knowledge through education, you can invest and prosper like the wealthy.

Your Allocation Strategy

As I mentioned in the previous chapters, diversifying your investments is important. How you decide to diversify is ultimately up to you.

If you're unsure as to how to diversify, I would recommend consulting with a Certified Financial Planner (CFP). Make sure you work with someone who is a fiduciary. A fiduciary is someone who as an obligation to do what's in your best interest – not the interest of the company the work for. You'll usually have to pay more to work with a fiduciary, but it will pay off in the long run.

An Example Allocation Strategy

In general, my diversification strategy never changes. I am steadfast in diversifying both across multiple asset classes, and within individual asset classes.

What does change over time is the specific allocation of my investments across different types of assets. My allocation in different assets changes over time, depending on my needs at any given time and what I think the economic future holds.

In an effort to provide you with some ideas for how you could allocate your investments, I have provided some rough guidelines for how I generally allocate mine. Remember that your needs and beliefs may differ, just as mine change over time. Use the information I provide as an example only.

My Allocation Strategy

Here are the rough percentages of my investments that I allocate to various asset classes. The ranges I provide are general and not hard limits, and change over time depending on my needs and my outlook for the future.

- Cash: **15 – 25%**
- Stock market: **15 - 25%**
- Real estate: **15 - 25%**
- Farmland: **15 - 25%**
- Lending: **5 - 10%**
- Precious metals: **10 - 15%**
- Cryptocurrency: **10 - 15%**
- Collectibles: **2 - 5%**
- Other: **3 - 10%**

Do What's Best For You

As I've stated before, you need to do what's best for you. There's not a single allocation strategy that's right for everyone, so do your research and invest wisely according to your risk tolerance, knowledge, and ability.

Onwards

Up unto this point I've covered asset types, diversification and allocation strategies, and liquidity. The next step is the fun step – assets! I'll take you through some major asset classes and describe what I think the pros and cons are of each. Let's get going!

Perpetual Wealth

Section 5

-

Assets For Building And Preserving Wealth

Perpetual Wealth

Chapter Thirty-Two
Cash

All Hail The King

Cash is king. There's no other asset that has the liquidity of cash, because cash is the definition of liquidity itself. Aside from providing for everyday expenses, having cash on hand (in a bank account) is important for:

- Emergency funds
- Opportunity funds

Emergency funds provide you with a reserve for when things go wrong, and opportunity funds allow you to purchase assets when the price is right.

Saving Is Losing

Here's the problem with cash... When you leave money in the bank, it is worth less and less over time. Inflation eats away at the purchasing power of your money, even if your bank account balance doesn't change.

Most people are taught to save money, but are unaware of the downside risk associated with cash. By failing to understand inflation and it's negative effect on cash holdings, many people end up losing out in the end.

That is not to say that saving is bad – you just have to employ it sparingly. Keep enough cash in your bank accounts for living expenses, emergency funds, and opportunity funds. Any remaining cash above your allocation limits should be deployed to investments that increase your wealth.

Diversifying Cash

I never keep all my cash in one bank. There are multiple reasons for this, including threats due to:

- Identity thieves and hackers
- Bank failures
- Lost or stolen debit cards or checks

By splitting my money across multiple banks, I have greater resiliency from problems that I may face in the future.

For example, if my debit card number gets stolen (as it has in the past), I have to wait several days for a replacement card with a new number to arrive. If I have multiple accounts, each with it's own card, my purchasing power is not diminished during that period.

The risk of identity thieves or hackers accessing my banking funds and emptying my account is reduced when I split money across multiple banks. Even though there is a larger attack vector (e.g. more bank accounts mean a higher chance of an attack), a single attack would not expose my entire bank balance to loss.

The Hidden Danger Of Banks

Another reason I split my cash holdings across multiple banks is to protect myself against a bank failure. Most people think I'm crazy for thinking a bank could fail, but I remember what happened during the financial crisis of 2008. I saw banks fail, I saw the government bail them out, and I saw what happened afterwards.

What most people don't know is that the banking laws changed after the financial crisis. If a bank fails in the future, the government might not step in to recover and protect the depositors (e.g. everyone who has a checking or savings account) like it did in 2008.

What's on the books now is the concept of bail-ins. What a bail-in means is that anyone who has money deposited at a bank might lose some or all of their money if the bank fails. If the banks decide to provide risky loans and fail as a result, we get to pick up the tab. Sounds fair, right? I didn't think so.

That's why I don't trust any single bank with all of my cash. I split my cash over multiple banks and I make sure each account stays below the old FDIC protection limits of $100,000.

Cash On Hand

I always keep some physical cash on hand for emergencies or unexpected circumstances, and I highly recommend to others that they do the same. In a time where most people rely on their debit card or credit card for purchases, it seems fewer and fewer people see the value in physical cash.

I've learned the hard way that having physical cash on hand is a lifesaver when unexpected circumstances arise. I don't keep a safe full of cash like you see in the movies, and I don't recommend others do either. It's too much of a security risk and there's no real need for it.

Keeping some cash in your wallet or purse allows you to purchase gas or food in a pinch if power and communication lines are out due to a storm or other blackout. In those situations, replying solely on a debit card or credit card isn't going to get you very far.

I also keep about a week's worth of cash for basic expenses (e.g. food and gas) in a safe place. That ensures I can purchase the necessities of life if a longer-term power outage strikes my local area.

No Interest

Most banks don't pay much of anything in terms of interest on cash in a standard checking a savings account. There are a few banks that offer high-interest checking accounts that provide 2% or more interest per year. That allows your cash to at least keep up with (or close to) normal inflation.

One of the companies I like for a high yield savings account is Wealthfront (wealthfront.com). As of the time of writing, they are offering an account with 2.57% interest.

Interest rates and companies often change, so your best bet on finding a high-interest checking or savings account is to search the Internet. Make sure to read reviews before you proceed with opening an account with any bank.

Fake Money

The cash we know and use on a daily basis is what is referred to as fiat currency. That basically means that it only has value because we believe it has value.

Money is just a means of transferring value between individuals and companies in exchange goods and services. There's no intrinsic value in money itself. There is, however, value in the things that money can buy.

Unlike other assets, cash isn't really a solid asset. That's because it's not something that has intrinsic value. As Robert Kiyosaki puts it, cash is "fake money". Grant Cardone says "cash it trash". These are both true statements in my opinion.

Cash is, however, extremely useful as a method of exchanging assets and purchasing things. It is the intermediary exchange between things of value. Thus, having cash in your bank account in excess of what's required to support your lifestyle is good, as it gives you the flexibility to acquire other assets easily.

Leaving too much money in the banks is risky, due to inflation, but that's something we all have to live with. You can counter the risk of inflation by investing the majority of your cash in assets that provide cash flow.

From a high level perspective, cash is not what makes you wealthy. Instead, assets – particularly assets that cash flow - make you wealthy.

My Cash Strategy

I typically allocate 15-25% of my net worth in cash, although this varies from time to time. This allocation provides me with a sufficient emergency fund to weather economic storms and an opportunity fund that is sufficiently large to acquire new assets when the price is right.

I diversify my cash as follows:

- Physical cash
    - Wallet or purse (walking around money)
    - Safe place (1 week's worth of basic expenses)
- Digital cash
    - Multiple banks and bank accounts

How you diversify your cash, and how much of your total assets that you allocate to cash will depend on your needs and objectives.

Why Cash Is Good, Not Evil

When you keep some of your money in the bank, you are ensuring that you have an emergency buffer for yourself and your family. That is good. By doing so, you are also prepared to make additional investments that can help provide you with a secure financial future. That is good.

Additionally, through the magic of fractional reserve banking, your bank will magnify the money you deposited and will be able to offer mortgages and car loans to people that need them. Thus, by keeping money in the bank, you are helping families achieve their American Dream. That is good.

Perpetual Wealth

Chapter Thirty-Three
Stocks

Market Maker

Most people are at least somewhat familiar with the stock market and the basic concepts involved in stock market investing. That's because the main focus of investing today revolves around retirement planning through 401ks that are offered through an employee's company.

However, most people aren't aware of two distinctly reasons (and methodologies) for investing in the stock market. They are:

- Price appreciation
- Cash flow

Most people simply focus on the price of a stock appreciating (increasing) over time. They hope the price of their stock holdings increases so they can realize a gain when they go to sell it.

This is a gamble, as the price is not always guaranteed to go up. Additionally, if a stock market crash or correction occurs shortly before they need to start selling their stock, the value of their stock holdings is severely diminished.

While the poor and middle class focus on appreciation, the wealthy view appreciation in value as a bonus, rather than a guarantee when it comes to investing. The wealthy know that cash flow is king.

Cash Flow

You can easily achieve cash flow from stocks if you invest in what are called dividend stocks. Dividend stocks are stocks that pay you earnings (dividends) on a regular basis – usually quarterly.

Different companies issue dividends at different times, so if you own dividend stocks from multiple companies, you can often achieve regular monthly cash flow from your dividend stocks.

I much prefer dividend stocks over non-dividend stocks, as dividend stocks provide ongoing cash flow from my principal investment.

Even though the price of dividend stocks may decline during economic downturns, it is likely that some level of cash flow would continue. When I don't need the cash flow for expenses, I can reinvest the dividends back into the dividend stocks. By doing this, I can leverage the power of compounded earnings to increase the cash flow capacity of my stock portfolio.

Aristocrats

When investing in dividend stocks, it's important to choose stocks wisely. New dividend investors often get seduced by stocks that offer a high dividend, completely unaware that high dividends are often a sign that a company could be overleveraged by debt.

A general rule of thumb when it comes to investing in dividend stocks is to invest in well run companies that have a long history of paying dividends. Stocks that offer dividend yields of more than 4% should be examined closely, as it can be a sign the company is trying to lure new investors in before they drop the dividend earnings.

Well-run companies that have offered consistently increasing dividends over a long period of time are referred to as the "Dividend Aristocrats". Wikipedia has a list of these companies at:

https://en.wikipedia.org/wiki/S%26P_500_Dividend_Aristocrats

Dividend Tax Treatment

A fantastic feature of dividend earnings is that you can achieve capital gains tax rates on your earnings if you receive what are called "qualified" dividends. Qualified dividends are essentially dividend payments that you receive from stocks that you've owned for several months.

There are some important rules and exceptions as to what determines a dividend earning to be qualified or not.

Investopedia has a great article that describes the rules for and tax treatment of qualified dividends at:

https://www.investopedia.com/terms/q/qualifieddividend.asp

Understanding dividend tax treatment is important – especially if you want to become a serious dividend investor. Check with a CPA for details on tax treatment of dividends as it relates to your personal situation.

Buy The Company

Many people view stocks as simply a stock ticker and a price. I believe, as other successful investors do, that you should view each stock as a company. After all, when you buy a company's stock you are a partial owner of that company.

With that in mind, it only makes sense to invest in stocks when you believe in the companies behind them. Don't be enticed to buy a stock that you don't understand just because you've heard it has huge potential for earnings or growth. Research each company and understand what they do and how they operate before you buy their stock.

Index Investing

If you're investing in the stock market for growth, a smart move to consider would be to invest in stock market index funds. Index funds track the overall performance of the stock market and have historically performed better than individually picked stocks.

Billionaire investing icon Warren Buffet believes in index funds so much that he has even gone so far as to have advised investors to put as much as 90% of their stock investments into index funds.

Vanguard offers some of the most highly rated index funds available. If you're looking to invest in the stock market for growth, I would encourage you to investigate index funds from Vanguard, Fidelity, and others that might fit well in your stock portfolio.

Buying Stocks

There are a number of different options for investing in the stock market. In recent years, several new companies have created platforms that make investing easy.

Some of the platforms that I recommend you investigate include:

- Betterment (betterment.com)
- Wealthfront (wealthfront.com)
- Schwab Intelligent Portfolios (hg.schwab.com)
- M1 Finance (m1finance.com)
- Robinhood (robinhood.com)
- Acorns (acorns.com)

Some platforms focus solely on growth investing, while others allow you the freedom to select individual stocks, which is ideal for dividend investing.

Some brokerage accounts that I recommend you investigate for investing in individual stocks include:

- Fidelity (fidelity.com)
- TD Ameritrade (ameritrade.com)

You'll have to evaluate the options that are available to you and make a determination as to what options to pursue based on your needs and goals.

Liquidity

One of the great things about stocks is that they are highly liquid. It's easy to sell them when you want. Like any investment, though, the price at what you can sell them for varies.

The high level of liquidity that stocks offer is one of the main reasons they're attractive to investors.

My Stock Investing Strategy

I split my stock market investing strategy between growth investing and dividend investing – typically 30% towards growth and 70% towards dividend.

Furthermore, I utilize a mix of robo-advisor platforms and self-directed investing platforms to diversify across strategies and brokerages.

For growth investing, I use the following robo-advisor platforms that auto-adjust stock, bond, and mutual fund investments:

- Betterment (betterment.com)
- Wealthfront (wealthfront.com)
- Schwab Intelligent Portfolio (hg.schwab.com)

For buying individual stocks for the purpose of dividend investing, I use the following sites/platforms:

- Fidelity (fidelity.com)
- TD Ameritrade (ameritrade.com)
- M1 Finance (m1finance.com)

Why The Stock Market Is Good, Not Evil

When you invest money in the stock market, you're putting your money to work for you and you're investing in your future financial security. That's good.

When you buy stocks, you're providing capital to businesses that allows them to expand, provide jobs, produce valuable goods and services, and improve our world through innovation. That's good.

Perpetual Wealth

Chapter Thirty-Four
Lending

Be The Banker

You've likely had to borrow money at some point in your life - whether it was for a mortgage, car loan, student loan, or credit card. When you look out a loan or line of credit, you became obligated to pay the lender back both the principal that was borrowed and any interest that accrued on that principal.

Peer-To-Peer (P2P) lending is turning the tables on the banking system for investors. P2P lending is a type of crowdfunding that allows individuals and businesses to bypass banks and go directly to investors for loans. This provides individual investors with the opportunity to invest their money and receive interest payments from borrowers.

Risks

There are always risks with any type of investment. P2P lending is no different in that respect. Loans given to individuals and businesses are generally unsecured, which means the main risks to investors come in the form of the borrower defaulting.

If the borrower defaults on an unsecured loan, they won't lose their house, car, or business. Instead, their credit rating will be negatively impacted. Defaults tend to rise during economic downturns, so you should expect to see higher than normal losses in your P2P lending investments during those times.

It should be noted that it is usual to have some percentage of your lending portfolio default, even in good economic times.

Platforms

There are four main P2P lending platforms that I've used. They include:

- StreetShares (streetshares.com)
- Lending Club (lendingclub.com)
- Prosper (prosper.com)
- Upstart (upstart.com)

StreetShares provides loans to small businesses (with a focus on veteran-owned businesses), while the other platforms focus on personal loans to individuals. StreetShares and Lending Club are available to everyone, while Prosper and Upstart are available only to accredited investors.

Liquidity

In general, the liquidity of P2P lending is somewhat low. The reason for that is because you are putting your money to work by lending others money. When you do that, you are giving borrowers a certain period of time (typically 3 years or more) to do so. As such, you can't ask for the entire principal back whenever you want.

If you want to exit your positions in your lending platforms (e.g. get your money out), you would need to disable any auto-invest feature in the platform and withdraw your money as the loans are paid off. This can take several months or years, depending on the length of notes (loans) that you've invested in.

StreetShares has a fairly high liquidity level compared to the other platforms. With StreetShares, you can withdraw your entire principal during your anniversary week. If you want your money out during any other time of the year, you pay a 1% fee on the money you're withdrawing.

Returns

StreetShares provides a 5% annual return when you invest money in their veterans bonds. That certainly beats any high-interest checking account you're going to find.

Returns offered by the other platforms can vary widely – often between 5% and 13%, depending on the types of loans you invest in.

Higher rates of return come from loans that are offered to individuals who have the lowest credit ratings and the biggest risk of default, as determined by the platform. Thus, high interest loans are most likely to default when compared to lower risk loans.

For that reason, I generally steer clear of high-risk loans that offer high returns. Instead, I choose to invest in lower return loans that are offered to borrowers with better credit ratings and a higher likelihood of being able to repay their loans. I believe this will help limit my losses due to defaults – especially during economic downturns.

As P2P lending is a fairly new asset class, it is unknown how stable or risky of an investment it will be in the long run – especially when the next economic downturn comes. P2P lending does, however, provide you with an option in diversifying your overall investment portfolio.

Cash Flow

The interest and earnings from your P2P lending (minus any losses due to defaults) is your cash flow. You typically earn and receive interest payments each month, which means you generally have positive cash flow each and every month.

My Lending Strategy

I typically allocate 5-10% of my net worth in P2P lending, depending on my short and medium-term goals.

I split my lending investments across different platforms, including:

- StreetShares (streetshares.com)
- Lending Club (lendingclub.com)
- Prosper (prosper.com)

- Upstart (upstart.com)

While the liquidity of StreetShares is fairly good, it is not that high for the other platforms listed. My loans across those platforms are usually in the form of 36 month notes (loans), which means it would take a full three years to get my entire principal out if I wanted to. Thus, I limit my investments in those platforms to a small amount that I could do without if things got tough.

Whether or not you decide to leverage P2P lending for your investments, as well as how you would choose to structure that portion of your overall investment portfolio, would obviously differ based on your specific needs and goals.

Why Lending Is Good, Not Evil

When you lend money and earn interest as a result, you are increasing your cash flow and able to provide a better life for yourself and family. That is good.

By providing loans to individuals, you are helping them to consolidate other higher interest debt or obtain something they need in life that they wouldn't otherwise be able to do on their own. That is good.

By providing loans to companies, you are helping businesses succeed, provide jobs, produce innovative products and services, and improve the overall economy. That is good.

Perpetual Wealth

Chapter Thirty-Five
Real Estate

A Space For Everyone

Everyone needs a place to live and work. And while buildings may grow old and be torn down and rebuilt, they aren't making any more of the land that the buildings sit on. This is what makes real estate a lucrative investment for many investors.

A Space For Everyone

Many people have made the mistake of thinking real estate always goes up in value. Unfortunately for millions of people, that line of thinking was proven incorrect during the financial crisis of 2008.

As with any investment, there is a risk over overvaluations in real estate due to economic bubbles. Real estate investors would be advised to keep this in mind before investing.

Types Of Real Estate

There are multiple types of real estate that you can invest in, including:

- Residential real estate
- Commercial real estate
- Manufactured homes
- Trailer parks
- Senior housing
- Student housing
- Storage units

Each type of real estate has its own set of pros and cons, and the location of the real estate, as well as market conditions, can have dramatic impacts on the value of real estate.

Ways To Invest In Real Estate

You can invest in real estate in multiple ways, including:

- Stocks
- REITs
- Direct purchase

Real Estate Stocks

You can invest in real estate through the stock market either directly through individual REITs or through index funds that track multiple REITs.

Some of the more popular REIT stocks include:

- Realty Income Corp (O)
- Digital Realty Trust (DLR)

- Welltower (WELL)
- Extra Storage Space (EXR)
- Public Storage (PSA)
- Getty Realty Corp (GTY)
- Senior Housing Properties Trust (SNH)
- Equity Lifestyle Properties (ELS)

Some of the more popular REIT and ETF index funds include:

- Vanguard Real Estate Index Fund (VGSIX)
- Vanguard Real Estate ETF (VNQ)
- Schwab U.S. REIT ETF (SCHH)
- iShares U.S. Real Estate ETF (IYR)
- iShares Global REIT ETF (REET)
- Fidelity MSCI Real Estate Index ETF (FREL)
- GraniteShares HIPS US High Income ETF (HIPS)

Investing Platforms

There are several platforms that make investing in real estate REITs. Some of my favorites include:

- Fundrise (fundrise.com)
- Rich Uncles (richuncles.com)

Real Estate Lending

In addition to real estate, investors also have the option of investing in short-term real estate loans.

Some of the platforms that offer real estate loan investing include:

- AlphaFlow (alphaflow.com)
- PeerStreet (peerstreet.com)

Investing in real estate lending has similar qualities as P2P lending when it comes to liquidity and borrower risk.

Direct Real Estate Investing

You can obviously choose to directly purchase real estate as part of your investment portfolio. When you do this, you can leverage the tax benefits of depreciation to reduce or potentially eliminate any taxes that would otherwise be due on the cash flow that you receive from rent.

The downside to owning real estate outright is that you either have to manage it yourself or hire someone to manage it for you. This is main reason I prefer investing in REITs rather than physical real estate.

Liquidity

Liquidity in real estate is, as a general rule, low. There are exceptions to this – especially if you buy a REIT stock or index fund. REIT stocks have high liquidity, where as non-stock REITs have low liquidity and may be illiquid until a specified holding period has been met.

If you own physical real estate outright, the liquidity is still low, as it takes time to find a buyer. Depending on market conditions, you might have a long period of time before you can sell your real estate.

Cash Flow

If you own real estate outright or invest in a REIT, you generally have ongoing rental income or dividends. That is your cash flow.

It should be noted that some real estate investments do not provide cash flow. Instead, some focus solely on the possibility of capital gains through appreciation.

My Real Estate Investing Strategy

I usually invest 15-25% of my net worth in real estate. My investments are split across:

- REITs
- Stocks
- Physical real estate

I also invest across different types of real estate, including:

- Residential real estate
- Commercial real estate
- Student housing
- Senior housing
- Manufactured homes

- Storage units

Fundrise (fundrise.com) is far and above my favorite investing platform. I especially appreciate the transparency that the Fundrise CEO has in regards to investing, as it gives me some level of assurance that the company is cognizant of the overall economy.

Why Investing In Real Estate Is Good, Not Evil

When you invest in real estate, you're providing people with a place to live and work. That is good.

Chapter Thirty-Six
Farmland

Feed The Need

Farmland is one of the assets that humanity can't live without. We're dependent on farmland to produce the food we all need to survive. Since farmland is limited (e.g. no one's creating more land), the scarcity of land presents an opportunity for investment.

Ways To Invest In Farmland

There are three main ways to invest in farmland:

- Farmland REITs
- Personal farmland ownership
- Fractional farmland ownership

Farmland REITs

Buying farmland through REITs is perhaps one of the easiest ways to invest a portion of your net worth in farmland.

Two popular REIT stocks that can be purchased easily include:

- Gladstone Land Corporation (LAND)
- Farmland Partners Inc. (FPI)

Both of these stocks offer dividends at the time of writing, so they provide cash flow as well as the potential for appreciation.

Personal Farmland Ownership

Another option for buying farmland yourself or through your company is to actually purchase a physical piece of land. Farmland that's for sale can be found on a number of sites, including:

- LandAndFarm.com
- LandWatch.com
- LandLeader.com

The benefit to owning farmland outright is that you have ready access to a physical asset. You can walk the land, feel the dirt, and see its value for yourself. The downside to owning land outright is that you have to manage leasing it to farmers and you have lower liquidity than REITs if you want to sell it.

Fractional Farmland Ownership

Another option for buying physical farmland is to invest alongside other investors in a plot of land. This is referred to as fractional ownership. Two companies that offer this type of farmland investing include:

- AcreTrader (acretrader.com)
- American Farm Investors (americanfarminvestors.com)

AcreTrader offers fractional ownership in farmland and provides investors with an exit date on their ownership interest. Individual farmland listings often offer a 3-10 year ownership hold, so your investment is locked in for a period of time. In addition to cash flow from farmland rentals, investors have the potential to realize gains from farmland appreciation during their holding period.

American Farm Investors (AFI) offers fractional ownership in syndicated farmland investments that are held in limited liability companies (LLCs). Investing through AFI is more of a buy-and-hold, perpetual investment. Investors receive cash flow from their investments, but investments are generally illiquid, unless a majority of members vote to sell the farmland or one member agrees to buy another member's units.

Liquidity

The liquidity of farmland REITs is very high. They can be bought and sold as easily as individual stocks.

The liquidity of physical farmland can be fairly low. If you personally own farmland, you have to sell it and find a buyer. If you're a fractional owner in a farmland investment, your investment may be illiquid altogether or restricted to a future sale date.

Cash Flow

Farmland REITs often provide dividends and physical farmland ownership usually provides rental income if it's rented out to farmers to grow crops. Those dividends and rental income are your cash flow.

My Farmland Investing Strategy

I typically invest 15-20% of my net worth in farmland. My investments are split across:

- Farmland REITs
- Fractional farmland ownership

Why Investing In Farmland Is Good, Not Evil

When you invest in farmland, you're supporting a resource that gives farmers the means to produce the food we all need to survive. That is good.

Chapter Thirty-Seven
Precious Metals

Meet The Ruler

Whoever has the gold makes the rules. That's the golden rule of gold and that's why kings and countries have held and continue to hold gold in their war chests. And it's why gold has served as one of the ways wealthy families have preserved their wealth across generations.

Relic Or Hedge

There are many people that believe that gold and other precious metals are barbaric relics of the past. They eschew precious metals and instead favor other more "modern" asset classes.

What these doubters choose to ignore is the fact that gold has a long, proven history as being a secure store of wealth and hedge against economic crises. From my point of view, just because something's old does not detract from its value. I like assets that have a long track record of performance.

Gold doesn't really participate in (e.g. see big gains) during economic booms or when the US dollar is strong. Instead, gold shines when there is economic chaos and when the dollar is weak. That is why gold is used a hedge against chaos, crisis, and disaster. It helps preserve and protect wealth in troubling times.

Central Store

What many people fail to understand is that gold has long been used to provide concrete backing to a country's currency. Even though there are no countries that currently have a gold-backed currency, countries continue to believe in the value of gold. Central banks from countries all around the world store gold as a store of value and an asset of last resort.

Several countries – notably Russia and China – have been accelerating their acquisition of gold reserves in recent years. Many experts believe they are doing this to hedge against a weakening dollar and to gain an advantage in the ongoing currency wars.

The topics of reserve currencies, currency wars, and central bank reserves are beyond the scope of this book. If you are interested in learning more about these topics, and why experts view gold as the ultimate hedge, I would urge you to read books written by Mike Maloney, Jim Rickards, and Nomi Prins. Additionally, Mike Maloney has a terrific YouTube channel where he regularly educates people on economics, precious metals, and the economy.

Real Money

Gold is often referred to as "real" money in a world dominated by fiat currency. That is due to its historic track record of being a real store of value and a protection mechanism against runaway money printing.

The Founding Fathers of the United States were keenly aware of the power of gold and the danger of fiat currencies. So much so, in fact, that the US constitution specifically designates gold and silver as the only legal money for the country.

Every single fiat currency in history has fallen to a value of zero eventually and it is highly likely that will continue in the future. That is why so many people value "real" money like gold. Robert Kiyosaki calls gold "God's money" and fiat currency "government's money".

More Than One

Gold isn't the only precious metal that you can invest in. The main metals that people usually invest in include:

- Gold
- Silver
- Platinum
- Palladium

Use Cases

In addition to providing a store of value, precious metals are used in:

- Electronics
- Batteries

- Medical therapies
- Manufacturing

Investment Methods

There are four main ways people invest in and obtain precious metals:

- Physical coins and bars
- Allocated storage
- Segregated storage
- ETFs

Each method has its pros and cons. I'll cover these in more detail below.

Physical Possession

Many gold "bugs" (proponents) profess that people should own and take possession of physical gold. They believe in the "if you can't hold it, you don't own it" philosophy.

While I believe this perspective has merit, there are huge security risks with doing so. Additionally, there is a relatively low liquidity rating with physical metal and selling physical gold presents another security risk.

There are multiple formats and weights of physical precious metals you can buy if you wish to do so. They include:

- Whole and fractional ounce coins

- Whole and fractional ounce bars

Experts recommend that investors looking to allocate a portion of their investments in physical precious metals should stay away from what are called numismatic coins and focus simply on bullion coins and bars. Numismatic coins are more of a collector item and carry high premiums in comparison to bullion.

If you're looking to purchase physical precious metals, check out the following dealers who have gotten high reviews:

- APMEX (apmex.com)
- GoldSilver (goldsilver.com)
- JM Bullion (jmbullion.com)

Allocated Storage

Allocated storage refers to having a company store your precious metals for you. Companies that provide allocated storage have vaults, security guards, and auditors that regularly verify precious metals are where they should be.

When you buy precious metals in allocated storage, you are essentially getting a percent ownership over the metals that are stored in a vault somewhere. You don't have specific ownership over a specific bar of gold, but you do have ownership of a percentage of the total metal stored.

Allocated storage is akin to saying "Joe owns X amount of gold and it's part of the pile of gold that's stored over there".

Allocated storage provides security and liquidity, but it does come with a cost. Investors who use allocated storage should expect to pay a monthly, quarterly, or annual fee for their precious metals holdings.

If you're interested in investing in allocated precious metals storage, I would encourage you to investigate the following companies:

- Hard Assets Alliance (hardassetsalliance.com)
- APMEX (apmex.com)
- GoldSilver (goldsilver.com)

Segregated Storage

Segregated storage is similar to allocated storage, but with a clear delineation of which gold belongs to whom. It's akin to saying "Joe owns X amount of gold and it's that specific bar over there with serial number ABC".

Segregated storage is appropriate for investors who want the highest level of assurance that their precious metals are theirs and theirs alone. In return for this added assurance and the overhead of keeping track of separate metals lots, fees for segregated storage are generally higher than those for allocated storage.

If you're interested in investing in segregated precious metals storage, I would encourage you to investigate GoldSilver (goldsilver.com).

ETFs

Another way to invest in precious metals is to buy precious metals ETFs on the stock market.

Gold bugs are often adamantly against precious metals ETFs, as the ETFs are often leveraged and there is not a direct relation of $1 worth of ETF to $1 of precious metal. This is the reason many experts are skeptical of using ETFs as a way of investing in precious metals.

I would agree with the experts on this point, with a few exceptions. There are some ETFs that are backed by allocated gold. One of my favorites is the AAAU ETF.

The AAAU ETF was introduced in 2018 by the Perth Mint of Australia and is backed by allocated gold. That provides me with a great deal of confidence that investing in AAAU is a wise choice if going with the ETFs.

Despite potential downsides with regards to leverage, ETFs are as easy to buy as stocks and have the same high liquidity.

Liquidity

The liquidity of physical precious metals that you have in your possession is fairly low. Converting them to cash requires selling them to a local coin shop, online precious metals dealer, or an individual. Thus, selling physical precious metals will take some time and also carries some risk of loss or theft.

The liquidity of precious metals stored in allocated or segregated is fairly high because the storage and management company is in possession of the metals and knows their value. This is one of the main reasons I like allocated and segregated storage.

Although the price you can sell them for will vary, precious metals have historically always held some value and are unlikely to go to value of zero.

The liquidity of precious metals ETFs is fairly high, as they can be sold just like a stock and converted to cash very quickly.

Cash Flow

Precious metals do not provide cash flow. Instead, investors hold them as a hedge against economic crises and for their (hopeful) price appreciation over time.

My Precious Metals Investment Strategy

I generally invest 10% of my net worth in precious metals. I do so for two main reasons:

- As a hedge against economic chaos
- As a liquid store of hard assets

Although I bought physical precious metals years ago when I first started investing, I have long since converted all my precious metal investments to allocated storage and ETFs. The main reasons I have done this are:

- **Security**. Armed guards and huge vaults protect my precious metals investments. I do not have to worry about the risk of theft.

- **Liquidity**. I like being able to quickly sell my precious metals for cash so I can purchase other assets when I find a good deal.

I diversify my precious metals investments across multiple storage companies and store my metals in multiple countries, including:

- The United States
- Switzerland
- Australia
- Singapore

Although the allocation of total metals I invest varies over time, I generally go with the following allocation across types of precious metals:

- 65% gold
- 20% silver
- 10% platinum
- 5% palladium

Allocated storage allows me to select various formats and weights of metals when I invest. The formats I invest in are:

- Bars (1oz, 10oz and larger)
- Coins (full or fractional ounces)

- Combibars (fractional grams)

The reason I allocate the way I do, in the locations I do, and with the different companies I do is for the following purposes:

- To hedge against storage company failure
- To hedge against potential country and location confiscation laws
- To allow me to sell small or large quantities as needed
- To provide maximum liquidity

My preferred choice for most of my precious metals investing is Hard Assets Alliance (HAA), which I believe offers a simple-to-use platform for buying and selling precious metals.

Your Choice

Although I believe strongly in the value of investing in precious metals, I understand it is not for everyone. If you are interested in doing so, do your research and make your own decisions based on your needs and long-term goals.

Why Investing In Gold Is Good, Not Evil

When you invest in precious metals, you're helping protect and preserve your wealth using a mechanism that has been proven over the centuries. That is good.

Chapter Thirty-Eight
Cryptocurrency

New Kid On The Block

Cryptocurrency is one of the newest asset classes to emerge on the scene. Cryptocurrency (or "crypto" as it is sometimes called) is an intangible, digital asset that can generally be used as a type of currency (e.g. means of exchange). Some cryptocurrencies can also be used to facilitate contracts, orders, and commerce.

Many experts tout cryptocurrencies as a method to helping free people from the restrictions and limitations of the current monetary system. This is due to the fact that cryptocurrencies are decentralized – e.g. no central bank or government controls them. It is for this reason that Robert Kiyosaki calls cryptocurrency "the people's money".

Leading Currencies

The most popular type of cryptocurrency is Bitcoin. Bitcoin was the first cryptocurrency to be developed and is the most widely held crypto asset among investors.

While there are over 2,000 other cryptocurrencies available (these are referred to as "alt-coins"), the leading ones other than Bitcoin are generally considered to be Ethereum and Litecoin.

Potential Upsides

Many people who are hard-core believers in cryptocurrency believe they have an immense upside. That is to say that many people expect their price to increase dramatically over time. Some people even claim that cryptocurrencies could see an increase of 1,000% or more from their price points as of mid-2019.

While immense price appreciations are a possibility, they are not a given. No investor should expect their investments to make such a large return. There is a risk that any investment in cryptocurrency could go to zero.

Exchanges

Cryptocurrencies can be bought, sold, exchanged, and stored on what are called "exchanges". Two popular exchanges that are available to US investors are:

- Coinbase (coinbase.com)
- Gemini (gemini.com)

Coinbase is the more popular of the two and offers the most features for buying, storing, and trading cryptocurrency.

Security

As with any digital asset, there is a risk of loss due to hackers and cybercriminals. Storing cryptocurrency on an exchange is widely considered to be a poor security practice and many experts in the crypto community recommend going with what are called offline wallets.

Offline wallets are simply a way for you to store some or all of your crypto assets on a device or medium that is inaccessible to the Internet. You can reduce the risk of loss due to hacking by utilizing offline wallets for your crypto storage.

When you buy cryptocurrency from an exchange, it's fairly easy and straightforward to transfer those crypto assets to your offline wallet. The details of how to accomplish that are beyond the scope of this book, but information can be readily found online.

Risks

While there is the potential for a significant upside to cryptocurrencies, there are a number of risks as well. Some of the main risks for crypto investors include:

- **Unproven asset**. Crypto is the newest kid on the block in terms of asset classes and does not have a long track record.

- **Risk of devaluation**. The price of cryptocurrencies is highly volatile. There is a risk that their value goes to zero and that all capital invested is wiped out.

- **Regulatory risks.** Government always lags behind innovation. It is likely that governments will regulate or restrict cryptocurrencies at some level in the future. This could result in cryptocurrencies being made illegal, highly restricted, or highly taxed.

Before investing in cryptocurrencies, you should consider and weigh the risks of doing so.

Liquidity

Cryptocurrencies are highly liquid if you store them on or transfer them to an exchange like Coinbase. In that case, you can exchange them for fiat currency (e.g. US dollars) fairly easily. The price at which you can sell them can vary widely, and cryptocurrency is currently a highly volatile asset, with prices being all over the board.

Cash Flow

Cryptocurrencies do not generate any cash flow. Investors hold them in the hopes they appreciate over time, so they can sell them for a profit at capital gains tax rates.

My Cryptocurrency Investment Strategy

I typically allocate 10-15% of my net worth in cryptocurrency and generally split the bulk of my crypto investments across:

- Bitcoin
- Ethereum
- Litecoin

Additionally, I diversify across exchanges and use both online and offline wallets.

Although I do invest in other "alt-coins" occasionally, I prefer to stick with what are generally considered the leaders.

Final Thoughts

Investing in cryptocurrency is fairly risky and speculative and should not be taken lightly. There's a good chance your entire investment could disappear if cryptocurrencies crash, fail, are heavily regulated, or banned outright. Consider these risks carefully before making any decision to invest in crypto.

Why Investing In Crypto Is Good, Not Evil

When you invest in cryptocurrencies, you're helping to support technology that looks to be the future of currency and transactions. And you're helping to support technology that has the potential to open up opportunities and free people from the limitations of the current monetary system. That is good - even though it's highly speculative.

Perpetual Wealth

Chapter Thirty-Nine
Collectibles

Collet $200 And Pass Go

An often-overlooked investment class is that of collectibles. Most people rarely think of collectibles when they're considering how to invest their money.

However, once you mention collectible investing to people, they often understand the value of collectibles. In fact, most people know someone in their life that has invested or is actively investing in collectibles.

One of the benefits of investing in collectibles is that you can enjoy using and/or admiring your investment. Driving an antique car or viewing a set of rare baseball cards is an experience that can be shared with others, whereas looking at the value of your stock portfolio doesn't have quite the same level of intrigue or enjoyment.

Types Of Collectibles

There are many different types of collectibles, including:

- Classic cars
- Antique and collector firearms

- Rare comic books
- Rare baseball cards
- Rare currency
- Rare stamps
- Rare books
- Rare sneakers/shoes
- Rare jewelry
- Rare coins
- Rare wine, champagne, and whiskey
- Diamonds, rubies, and other precious stones

Risks

There are several risks with investing in collectibles, including:

- **Risk of depreciated prices.** The market for your collectible might become oversaturated or depressed and you could end up losing money.

- **Risk of no market.** If the collectible is no longer of interest to others, you won't be able to sell it. Also, if government regulations make owning or transferring your collectible illegal, you won't be able to sell it.

- **Risk of loss.** You're going to have to store your collectible somewhere and protect it against theft, water damage, and fire. If it ends up getting lost, stolen, damaged, or destroyed, you're out of luck.

You should carefully weigh these risks before you start investing in collectible. Each type of collectible will have it's own set of risks, market, and security requirements.

Tried And True

When investing in collectibles, I always make it a point to stick with the tried and true. Newly hyped collectible crazes like the Beanie Baby craze in the 1990s resulted in many people losing a significant portion of their investments. In order to counter the risk of losing money in collectibles, I stick with those types that have a long track record of storing value and appreciating in price over time.

Returns

Returns for collectibles are going to vary widely and will depend on the type of collectible you own, how long you've held it, and what kind of market there is for the item when you go to sell it. It's quite possible that there will be no market when you try to sell a collectible, so keep that in mind before you buy one.

If you hold a collectible for more than a year, you should be able to get long-term capital gains treatment on the sale. You should consult with you CPA as to your particular tax situation and whether or not you would qualify for long-term capital gains tax treatment.

Liquidity

Liquidity for collectibles is going to be somewhat low. It often takes a significant amount of time to find a buyer for what you're selling, so collectibles don't have a high liquidity rating.

Depending on what you're selling and when you're selling it, your collectible might go fast. But don't count on that when you get into collectibles. They market for your collectibles can change and you could be left holding something that you can't sell.

Cash Flow

There generally isn't any cash flow when it comes to collectibles. Instead, collectibles are part of your portfolio income and you are hoping for an appreciation in price before you sell it.

My Collectibles Investment Strategy

I typically allocate less than 5% of my net worth to collectibles and usually split my collectible investments across:

- Collector comic books
- Collector cars
- Rare books

If The Shoe Fits

Whether or not investing in collectibles is appropriate for you, and to what extent if any you do invest, will depend on your needs and goals.

Why Investing In Collectibles Is Good, Not Evil

When you invest in collectibles, you are investing in a hard, tangible asset that can be used, admired, and appreciated by yourself and others. That is good.

At the same time, you are providing financial capital to the companies and individuals that you bought the collectible from. This allows them to support their employees and families. That is good.

Perpetual Wealth

Chapter Forty
Other Alternative Assets

There are many other types of investment asset classes that I haven't covered in this book. Some examples include:

- Angel Investing
- Businesses
- Timberland
- Undeveloped land
- Oil and Gas Exploration
- Fine Art
- Lawsuit Settlement Financing
- Marine Vessel Deconstruction

There are literally hundreds of different asset classes out there. New investors often don't get involved in these types of investments because:

- They don't know they exist
- They aren't an accredited investor
- They don't have the connections
- They don't have the capital to invest

If you are an accredited investor and you do have free capital to invest, there's an easy option for you to get started in a few additional types of alternative investments.

YieldStreet (yieldstreet.com) is a relatively new company on the block that makes investing in alternative assets fairly simple. Investments through YieldStreet typically yield an **8%-15%** return each year. That's an amazing return compared to many other investments out there.

But there's a catch. You have to be an accredited investor to join YieldStreet and participate in investments that they offer. Remember when I said some of the best investments seem to be offered to accredited investors only? This is an example of that in action.

That's why I recommend everyone work on increasing their income and net worth so they can qualify as an accredited investor.

If you're already an accredited investor, visit **yieldstreet.com** to learn more about who they are and what types of investments are available.

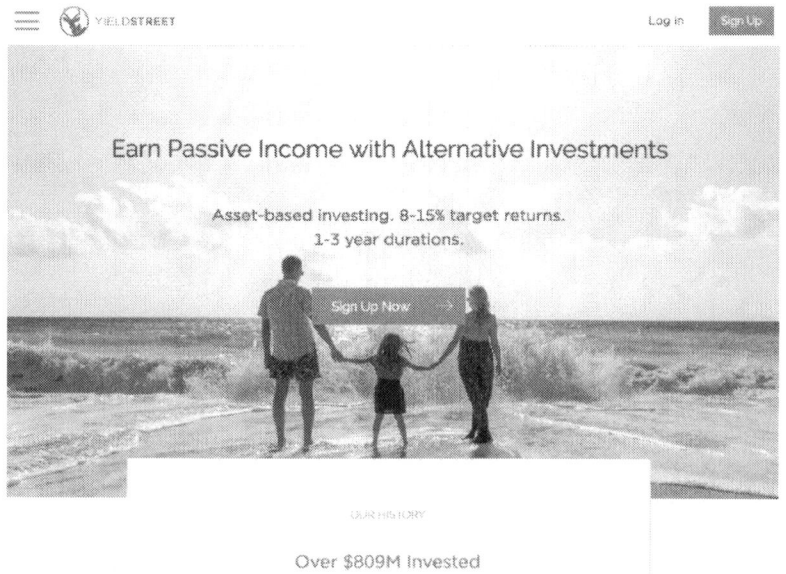

Returns

I've seen returns for alternative assets anywhere from 6%-15% per year. Returns will vary depending on what you invest in and some assets will focus on expected appreciation (capital gains), rather than (or in addition to) an annual yield. Make sure to review the details on any specific investments you're interested in to make sure they meet your expectations before you decide to invest.

Liquidity

With YieldStreet, the investments are illiquid. You have to hold the investments until they mature (often 6 months to 3 or more years).

Liquidity for alternative investments elsewhere will vary, although you should expect fairly low liquidity if any. Most alternative investments are illiquid until a specific exit date.

Cash Flow

With YieldStreet, the interest payments or earnings from investments is your cash flow. You typically earn and receive interest payments each month, which means you generally have positive cash flow each and every month.

Alternative investment elsewhere may product regular interest payments or earnings, which would constitute your cash flow.

My Alternative Investment Strategy

I typically allocate 3-10% of my net worth in alternative assets, depending on my short and medium-term goals.

I split my alternative investments across different asset classes, including:

- Marine Vessel Reconstruction
- Hotel Refinancing
- Real Estate Financing

Whether or not your invest in alternative assets, and to what extent if any you do, will depend on your needs and goals.

Why Investing In Alternatives Is Good, Not Evil

When you invest in alternative investments, you are diversifying your overall investment portfolio, which can give you a measure of protection against economic turmoil. That is good.

Section 6

-

Shake Your Money Maker

Perpetual Wealth

Chapter Forty-One
Generating Additional Income With High Efficiency

Money doesn't reward hard work. Money rewards value.

That's an extremely important concept to remember. Most people think money rewards education, skills, time, and hard work. It does not. Money rewards value.

Most people trade their time for money. They spend most of their adult life slaving away at a job they don't like. They spend all or more of the income they earn on things that don't increase their wealth and they are forced into a position where they always need to earn more to keep up with their ever-increasing expenses.

This cycle continues in perpetuity until they retire, at which point they have to live off the government or their sorely underfunded retirement accounts.

This is the definition of the rat race. This is definition of financial slavery. This is not what you want your life to be like.

In order to get ahead in life, escape the rat race, and secure your wealth in perpetuity, you must live below your means, invest wisely in assets that cash flow, and refrain from spending, selling, or otherwise diminishing your investment assets.

If you want to escape the rat race as quickly as possible, you need to increase the money you have available for investments. You can do this by decreasing your expenses and/or increasing your income.

You can only decrease your expenses so far, but you don't have any upper limit on the income you can bring in. Increasing your income is therefore the most effective way to generate additional money for purposes of investing.

Rather than trade your precious time for each dollar your earn, it is important to separate your time from the money you earn if you want to increase your income efficiently.

When you earn $40 per hour for each hour you work, you are limited as to how much total income you can generate. When you separate how much money you earn from the amount of time you work, there is no limit to the income you can generate. Instead, you have a potential for unlimited return. That is efficient.

How can you increase your income? Simple. Money rewards value.

The amount of value you provide someone determines how much they're willing to pay you. If you provide little value, they're likely to pay you a little money, if any at all. If you provide enormous value, they're likely to pay you a lot of money. Increasing the amount of value you provide others is the key to determining how high of an income you can achieve.

You can increase your value at your job by learning new high-income skills and putting them to work. High-income skills are skills that are strategic or highly specialized. These include management skills, financial skills, marketing skills, strategic thinking skills, and scarce skills such as software development.

If you acquire new skills, but do not use them in your job, they do you no good. You will not be able to increase your income much if you are not using your skills on the job. Unused skills may look good on a resume, but they provide no value to an employer and are a waste of time and effort. You need to use your skills to provide increased value to your employer if you want the best chance at increasing your earnings.

While using your skills to provide value at a job can increase your income, it cannot scale infinitely. You will always reach a cap in your earnings potential and will always be trading your time for money. This is not the most efficient way to earn money.

What you're looking for is maximum income for minimal effort. Making that happen requires maximum efficiency. Making that happen requires leverage. Making that happen requires planning and effort. Nothing in life is free. Everything takes effort. But some things come easier if you work smarter.

They key to creating high levels of income efficiently requires:

- **High value proposition**
- **Leverage**
- **Time value separation**

Let's talk about what those mean.

A **value proposition** is created when you know, have, or provide something that someone else needs or wants. When they want something you can provide, there exists a value proposition you can exploit to your benefit. The higher the value proposition and the higher the desire or need, the higher the potential for income.

Leverage involves using other people's money, knowledge, resources, systems, or emotions to accomplish something easier than it would be to do without.

Time value separation means that your income generating potential is not directly related to the amount of time you put into creating whatever it is that you are providing.

Here's an example of a money making machine that meets these criteria…

Writing A Book

Yes, writing a book. Writing a book is one method that can increase your income dramatically in an efficient manner. When you write a book:

- **You exploit a value proposition**. You write about something that you know more about than other people. You don't need to be the world's utmost expert on a subject – you just need to know more than some other people. Since the people that know less about your topic want to know what you know, they're likely to buy your book if they know about it.

- **You use leverage**. You're leveraging what you've learned from others when you write your book. You're leveraging a publisher and/or a publishing platform (like Amazon.com) to get your book out to the public.

- **You separate your time from the value created**. Writing a book will take time, but it will only take a certain number of hours. The number of books you can sell and the amount of income you can generate from the book is not directly tied to the time you put in. This allows for the possibility of an infinite return.

When I suggest writing a book to most people as a way to increase their income, I usually get a bunch of excuses as to why the can't. They say they're not an author, they're not an expert, and they don't have the time. These are all bullshit excuses and lies they tell themselves and others that ultimately hold them back from becoming wealthy.

Everyone is an author. Everyone writes emails and communicates to others via speech on a daily basis. You're already an author. You just probably haven't published a book yet.

Everyone has the same amount of time in the day. How you choose to spend it is up to you. If you want to become financially free and build perpetual wealth, you have to put in the time. You have to work after everyone else goes to sleep. You have to work early in the morning. You have to work on the weekends. There is no gain without pain.

Everyone is an expert on something because expertise is relative, not absolute. You may not be the world's utmost expert on any given topic, but you know more about it than some other people.

If you write about a topic that people are interested in, the people who know less about it than you do are your target market. You are a relative expert on the subject compared to them.

When it comes to choosing a title for your book, you need to leverage and exploit other people's emotions and basic desires.

For example, everyone generally wants more money, more time, more success, and more love. And we want it easier, faster, cheaper, and better. We're all greedy bastards.

Example book titles that exploit these desires and leverage emotions include:

- 10 Easy Ways For Single Moms To Make More Money
- How To Be A Successful Entrepreneur
- How To Build A Secure Retirement Nest Egg
- Find Your Soulmate In Five Simple Steps
- Get Rich And Live The Life You've Dreamed Of
- The 4-Hour Work Week
- The Millionaire Next Door
- Think and Grow Rich

Those are titles that exploit the desires and emotions of other people. There's nothing wrong with that. That's just how you get things done effectively and efficiently.

Other Options

Writing a book isn't the only efficient method of increasing your income. Here are a few other ways you can accomplish the same goal:

- Produce videos on YouTube and monetize the channel
- Write a software application
- Build a tutorial series
- Run a seminar or conference

All of those options have the same three attributes:

- Value proposition
- Leverage
- Time value separation

Get To Work

You can either make excuses or you can make more money. You can't do both. If you want to be financially free and build lasting wealth, you have to make the effort. No one is going to do the work for you. You have to do it. So if you decide more money is what you want, stop making excuses and get to work.

Perpetual Wealth

Section 7

-

Final Thoughts

Perpetual Wealth

Chapter Forty-Two
Final Thoughts

Think And Act Differently

Most people don't practice good money habits. Most people live paycheck to paycheck, trade their time for money, and don't save or invest at the rates they should. Most people buy the biggest house they can afford and have no money left over to acquire true wealth. Most people live for today and, as a result, sacrifice their financial future. Most people are screwed. Don't be like most people.

In order to build lasting, perpetual wealth, you need to think for yourself, take responsibility, and take action. If you focus your efforts on investing in assets that cash flow, you can create perpetual money machines that make you truly wealthy.

Build Wealth Consistently

When you get started on building your wealth machines, it can seem like an impossible task to achieve great wealth. If you put $100 into an asset that cash flows at a rate of 5% per year, you'll only get $5 per year in return. That's not going to feel like a big win to achieving great wealth.

However, the results get better over time as you increase your investment in wealth machines. Once you have $10,000 in an asset that has a 5% yearly return, you're bringing in $500 per year. If you have $100,000 in the investment, you're bringing in $5,000 per year. If you reach a million dollars in the investment, you're bringing in $50,000 per year. Assuming the returns are consistent, that's a perpetual return of $50,000 per year. That's amazing!

Be Patient

Remember to be patient with building your wealth. By leveraging time and the power of compounding returns through continual reinvestment, you can increase your wealth substantially.

Spend The Earnings, Not The Principal

Once you stop contributing new principal to your investments, it's important to limit your spending to the cash flow that's generated from the interest and earnings coming from your investments. By doing that, you never degrade your principal and you have perpetual wealth that can provide income over your lifetime.

Sell Smartly

If you decide to sell some of your assets, you can often achieve favorable tax rates if the assets qualify for capital gains tax rates. An important thing to keep in mind is that your capital gains tax rate can be 0% if your regular income (employment, interest, and rent earnings, etc) doesn't exceed the lowest tax bracket limits. You can achieve this by re-structuring your wealth machines so that regular income is limited to match this tax bracket limitation. Be sure to consult with your CPA for specific recommendations based on your financial situation.

Work Smarter Not Harder

Trading your time for money in a regular job is one of the most time-intensive ways to earn money. Focus your efforts on building streams of income using minimal effort for maximum impact.

Trust In The Process

Most people stress over money. In fact, it's one of their biggest worries in life and one of the leading reasons for divorce. Always remember that money is not worth sacrificing your quality of life.

Spend time learning about money, finance, and wealth and put into practice those strategies that you feel comfortable with. If you invest intelligently and consistently over time, your wealth will grow and you can rest easy knowing that your financial future is secure.

Do Good Things

As you build your wealth, make sure to do good things for others. That will help keep you grounded and provide much needed assistance to others that are in need of help. By donating your money (and/or time) to charitable causes, you are doing good for humanity and yourself. Nothing feels better than helping others out. People, relationships, and experiences are what life is all about – not money.

Teach Others

The greatest gift you can give to others is knowledge. As they say, if you give a man a fish, he eats for a day. If you teach a man to fish, he can feed himself for a lifetime.

There's only one thing missing from that – a greater truth that's been hidden… If you teach a man to invest in fishing companies, he can feed himself without having to do the work of fishing himself.

Once you have an understanding of financial literacy, how to build money machines, how to build lasting wealth, and the power and freedom that comes from that, I believe that you have an obligation to teach others how to do it for themselves.

You didn't come by all of the knowledge you have by yourself. Instead, you learned from others and from your own experiences. Teaching others who are willing to learn is one of the greatest things you can do with your life. Knowledge can elevate people, improve their lives, and help all of humanity.

Teaching is one of the greatest – if not <u>the</u> greatest – professions due to its enormous impact on the lives of others.

Best Wishes

I hope you found the information in the book useful to you. If you like it, please share it with your friends and family. If you have criticisms, please let me know so I can improve future publications.

I wish you all the best in your endeavors and your journey to achieving great wealth. Good luck and best wishes!

- Ethan Galstad

Perpetual Wealth

Section 8

Resources

Perpetual Wealth

References and Resources

Headed For The Cliff

2018 TransAmerica Center For Retirement report
https://www.transamericacenter.org/docs/default-source/retirees-survey/tcrs2018_sr_retirees_survey_financially_faring.pdf

Average retirement savings by age
https://www.investopedia.com/articles/personal-finance/011216/average-retirement-savings-age-2016.asp

Vanguard's "How America Saves 2019" report
https://institutional.vanguard.com/iam/pdf/HAS2019.pdf

GAO report on retirement assets
https://www.gao.gov/assets/690/687797.pdf

Average 401k balance by age
https://www.bankrate.com/retirement/average-401k-balance-by-age/

Wealthy Chicago residents on the hook for $2M in unfunded pension liabilities
https://wirepoints.org/wealthy-chicago-households-on-the-hook-for-up-to-2-million-in-debt-each-under-progressive-approach-to-pension-crisis/

Additional Resources

For more information about resources, useful links, and additional books and educational material, visit the ZeroToHero.co website at:

http://zerotohero.co

On that site you'll find free videos that cover various topics including finance and personal growth.

Recommended Reading

Here are just a few of the books that I believe would be useful in your understanding of finance, wealth, and investing. You can find all these books for sale at Amazon.com

**The Demographic Cliff:
How to Survive and Prosper During the Great Deflation Ahead**

Rich Dad's Prophecy

Think and Grow Rich

Recommended Reading Cont'd

Guide To Investing in Gold & Silver: Protect Your Financial Future

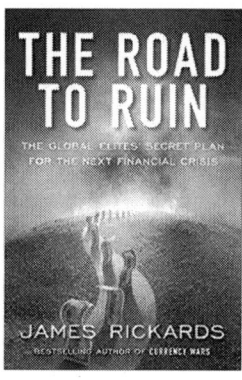

The Road to Ruin: The Global Elites' Secret Plan for the Next Financial Crisis

The Millionaire Next Door: The Surprising Secrets of America's Wealthy

Recommended Reading Cont'd

 **The Richest Man In Babylon**

 **The 4-Hour Work Week**

Think and Grow Rich

"Think and Grow Rich" is a phenomenal book written by Napolean Hill. It's not a new book by any means, but its messages are timeless. It's been said that millionaires re-read this book on a regular basis to remind themselves about its principles.

An essential message of the book is that "ordinary" people can obtain extraordinary outcomes if they just apply themselves, taking things step by step.

The ideas in the book extend far beyond just obtaining financial wealth and business success. You can use the principals to grow rich in compassion, courage, and abilities as well. If you don't want to take the time to read the book, you can watch the "Think And Grow Rich: The Legacy" movie on Amazon.com to get a synopsis of some of the book's core concepts.

I can't say enough about this book!

Zero To Hero Website

The official Zero To Hero website is online at:

http://zerotohero.co

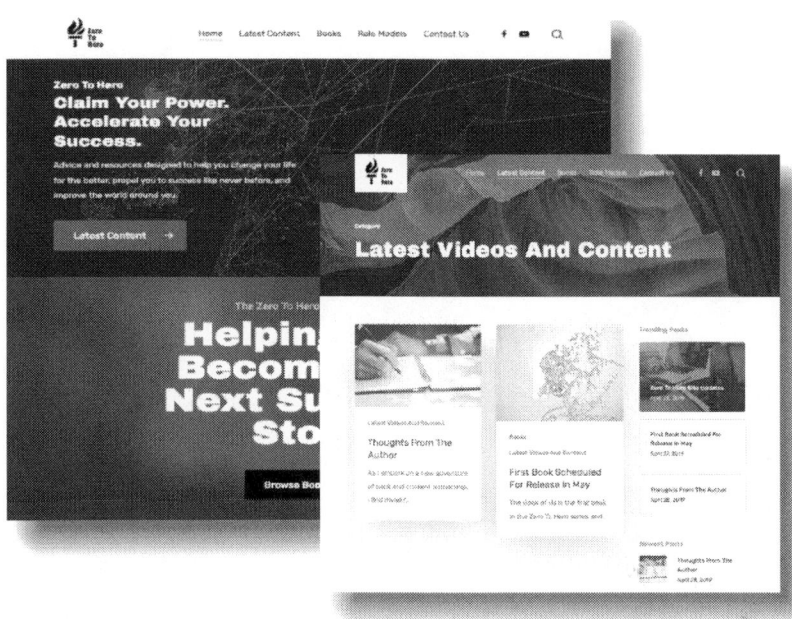

The website contains information on the latest book releases and features original videos that cover topics on finance, personal growth, inspirational stories, and ideas for improving our world.

Have a question about the book or have an idea for a new video? Use the contact page on the website to get in touch with me. I'd love to hear from you!

Inspiring Role Models

I'm inspired by many people (and many companies) and I consider them all to be role models for different reasons. I've put together a list of these people and companies on the Zero To Hero website at:

http://zerotohero.co/role-models

Below you'll find a short list of some of the people that inspire me and why. I would encourage you to write down your own list and see who inspires you. Follow their lead in your personal path to self-improvement and financial betterment, and you can achieve greater levels of success than you ever thought possible.

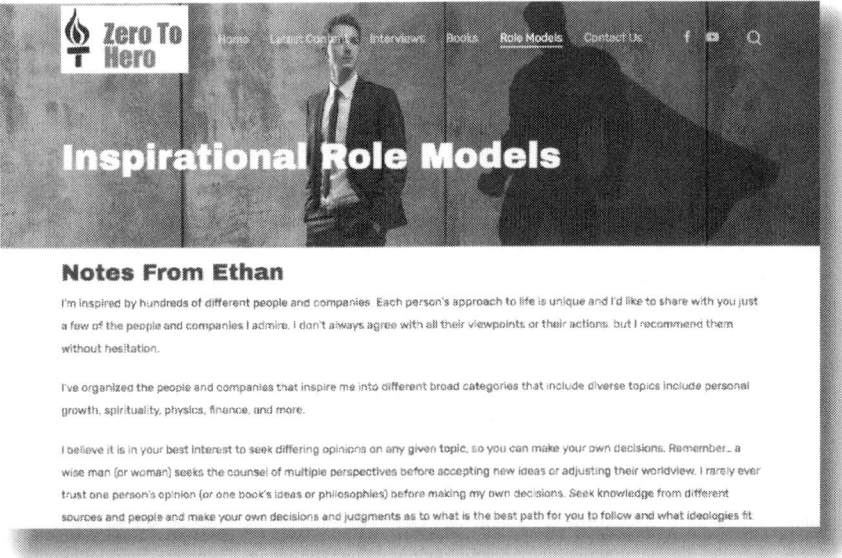

I'm inspired by:

My son.
His constant quest for learning reminds me of my childhood and inspires me to be the best father I can be.

The friends I have.
They support me in times of need and challenge me to grow.

The friends I've lost.
They forced me to look inside myself to see where I had to grow.

My parents.
Their dedication to teaching and caring for my sister and me will never be forgotten.

My doubters and competitors.
They help me to push forward harder. The race would be much less fun without them.

My team at Nagios.
Everyone in the company (present and past) has taught me so much. Thanks team!

Jeff Bezos.
For his vision and dedication into building Amazon.com into the powerful company that provides so many of us with an easier life. I'm especially grateful for the ease at which an independent-minded person such as myself can self-publish a book without searching for a publisher who believes in my ideas.

Elon Musk.
For his tenacity and dedication to building SpaceX and Tesla, while continually proving that you can overcome the doubters and achieve great heights. I love what you do and so do many others. After all, what young kid doesn't like rockets?

Richard Branson.
For building his empire of companies from its early humble beginnings as a record store.

Michael Dell.
For starting a well-respected technology company from his dorm room in college.

Warren Buffet.
For his phenomenal success and upbeat attitude that started from hard work and humble beginnings.

Bill Gates and **Steve Jobs**.
For building two amazing companies that have changed the world of computing forever.

The team at Hewlett-Packard.
For creating amazing technology solutions and an awesome "***Make It Matter***" video that is truly inspiring and perhaps the best company promo video I've ever seen.

The team at Goalcast...
Jay Shetty...
Tom Bilyeu of **Impact Theory...**
Nuseir Yassin of **NAS Daily...**
and **Prince EA**...
For providing inspiring messages that promote growth, understanding, and self-improvement.

Jim Kwik.
For his explanation of how our brains work and how we can unlock our full potential.

"Rich Dad" Robert Kiyosaki.
For teaching me the value of financial concepts and the importance of cash-flowing assets.

Mike Maloney of **GoldSilver.com**.
For his dedication to education people about the financial world.

Dan Peña (the 50 billion dollar man).
For his enormous successes and his continued dedication to teaching others his methods. And for the fact that he swears like me.

Dan Lok.
For his business and financial success and his dedication to teach.

Mark Moss from **Market Disruptors**.
For presenting complex ideas in a straightforward, humble, and no-nonsense manner.

William Hurley (whurley).
For providing me with inspiration as to what one person with dedication can accomplish. I admire you, my friend!

Alex Koffmann.
For being one of the best friends I could ask for. You've saved my ass more than once buddy!

Made in the USA
Coppell, TX
24 May 2020

26353662R00136